Publisher: English Language Products, LLC

Author and Creator: Curt Reese

Editor: John Fowler

Designer: Jeff St.Onge, StOngeCreative.com

© 2015 by English Language Products, LLC. All rights reserved. No part of this work may be reproduced or transmitted in any form or by any means electronic or mechanical, including photocopying and recording, or by any information storage or retrieval system without the prior written permission of English Language Products, LLC, unless such copying is expressly permitted by federal copyright law. Please address inquiries to Educational Permission, English Language Products, LLC, 1107-A Mason Avenue, Austin, TX 78721.

Printed in The United States of America

ACKNOWLEDGEMENTS

This project has taken 14 years to complete. Many people were involved in the testing of this product. These include: Meghan Ackley, Tony Anderson, Dara Chambers, Katie Cottier, Katherine Ellis, Sarah Episcopo, Carol King, Mary Kracklauer, Melissa Lee, Christine McCourt, Elizabeth Steinbach and Terri Wells.

PREFACE

This book and card game is a program designed to help you with speaking English conversation. While it was specifically designed to help students succeed in academic conversations, the phrases and moves are also useful in non-academic settings. The product has been employed at my university for speaking classes over the last 15 years, and used by numerous teachers as well as hundreds of students. The product has been well tested.

The origins of this book started in 1999. At that time, I took a job as an ESL instructor while I pursued graduate studies. My first class was a speaking course, part of which involved "moderated discussions." These are conversations about academic topics. Students took participant or leader roles, and they were supposed to use functional phrases for particular conversation moves. I was provided with a very brief list of a few conversational phrases and told to have students use them. This method did not work well for me.

Fortunately, I was able to take some courses on conversation analysis. I researched various conversation moves and phrases that go along with these phrases in academic literature as well as my own recordings of conversations. From this, I generated a list of functional phrases that go along with common conversational moves, and created a card game to go along with the phrases, in order to give students more structured practice of the phrases before attempting to use the phrases without any scaffolding. Several of my co-workers agreed to test the product in their own classes, and they provided me with useful feedback to my product.

THE CONVERSATION GAME

The Conversation Game: A Systematic Program for Mastering English Conversation

TABLE OF CONTENTS

Acknowledgements v
Preface vi

1 THEORY, OVERVIEW, & DIAGNOSTIC   **1**
    Objectives of this Chapter 1
    Theoretical Backing 1
    Conversation Analysis 2
    Vocabulary 2
    Cards 2
    Formulaic Language: The Two Levels of Conversation 3
    Elements of the Program 4
    Formulaic Phrases 4
    Topics 4
    Questions & Written Exercises 4
    Conversation Moves/Strategies: 5
    Pair Work & Group Work (Conversation Games) 6
    Variations/Drills 6
    Teacher's Role 6
    Diagnostic 7
        Topic #1: Public Smoking Bans 7

2 BASIC SKILLS FOR CONVERSATIONS   **11**
    Objectives of this Chapter 11
    Expressing Opinions, Agreeing and Disagreeing 11
    Expressions 12
    Turn-Taking Using Basic Expressions 12
        Topic #2: Learning a Language 13
    Preparation for Practice with Expressions 14
    Opening Up the Floor with Agreement 15
        Topic #3: World Language 16
    Buying Time with "In + I" 19
        Topic #4: Standardized English Tests 20

3 LEADING A CONVERSATION   **23**
    Objectives of this Chapter 23
    Expressions 24
    Role of the Leader 24

    Introducing a Topic 24
        Topic #5: Astrology 25
    Preparation for Leaders 27
    Moving the Discussion Along 28
        Topic #6: Feng Shui 29
    Concluding Conversations 32
        Topic #7: Dreams 32

4 ASKING FOR REPETITION & REPHRASING   35
    Objectives of this Chapter 35
    Asking for Repetition and Rephrasing 35
    Expressions 36
    Turn-Taking with Asking for Repetition and Rephrasing 36
        Topic #8: The Growing Problem of Obesity 36
    Softening the Blow with Two Repetition Phrases 39
        Topic #9: Obesity in the Workplace 40
    Buying Time with Two Rephrasing Phrases + Opinion 43
        Topic #10: Fat Tax 44

5 ELICITING PARTICIPATION & AVOIDING QUESTIONS   47
    Objectives of this Chapter 47
    Eliciting Responses and Avoiding Questions 47
    Expressions 48
    Basic Eliciting Participation & Avoiding Questions 48
    Turn-Taking with Eliciting Participation & Avoiding Questions .. 48
        Topic #11: Invasive Species and Exotic Pets 49
    Buying Time with Avoiding the Question + Opinion 52
        Topic #12: Global Warming 53
    Buying Time with "Avoiding the Question" + "In + I" 56
        Topic #13: The Ecological Impact of Green Energy 56

6 INTERRUPTIONS & MANAGING THE CONVERSATION   61
    Objectives 61
    Expressions 62
    Interrupting 62
        Topic #14: School Choice 62
    Going off on Tangents and Reining in Tangents 65
        Topic #15: Home Schooling 66
    Interrupting/Reining in Tangents/Moving the Discussion Along .. 69
        Topic #16: School Uniforms 70

7 EXTENDED TURNS — 73

- Objectives 73
- Expressions 74
- Opinion Runs 74
  - *Topic #17:* Face-Recognition Software 74
- Acknowledging and Minimizing Counterarguments 77
  - *Topic #18:* Google Earth 78
- Acknowledging and Minimizing Counterarguments II 80
  - *Topic #19:* Workplace Surveillance 81

8 CONFIRMING INTERPRETATIONS, CORRECTING MISUNDERSTANDINGS & AFFIRMING — 85

- Objectives 85
- Expressions 85
- Turn-taking with Confirming Understanding & Affirming 86
  - *Topic #20:* Psychotherapy 87
- Turn-taking with Confirming Understanding and Correcting Misunderstanding 89
  - *Topic #21:* Is Personality Inherited? 90
- Softening the Blow and Buying Time with Rephrasing 91
  - *Topic #22:* Mood Disorders and Creativity 93

9 ALGINING WITH OTHERS — 97

- Objectives 97
- Expressions 98
  - *Topic #23:* Unidentified Flying Objects (UFOs) 98
- Aligning with Positive First-Person Statements 101
  - *Topic #24:* Ghosts 101
- Aligning with Negative First-Person Statements 104
  - *Topic #25:* Astrological Prophesy 104

10 ASSESSING PROGRESS AND FURTHER PRACTICE — 109

- Objectives 109
- *Topic #26:* Plastic Surgery 109
- Written Assignment: Final Evaluation 112
- Individual WrittenAssignment 112

APPENDICES 113-126

THEORY, OVERVIEW, AND DIAGNOSTIC

OBJECTIVES OF THIS CHAPTER
- Understand the theoretical background of this method
- Gain an understanding of your conversational ability now

The Conversation Game is designed to help you with English conversation skills. Through this program, you should learn not only various conversation expressions that are effective on the meaning level for entering conversations, but you will also learn various conversation moves. By memorizing expressions for conversations and practicing them, you should be able to enter conversations with ease. This book is designed to help you quickly and easily participate in conversations in ways that are appropriate to speakers of American English.

THEORETICAL BACKING

In this book, I have treated conversation more as we typically treat grammar – to be taught explicitly – rather than 'free-form.' While I feel free-form may be beneficial depending on students' ability levels and other circumstances, we *infrequently* treat conversation as we treat grammar. Here, conversation has been broken down into various component parts, which can separately be examined, analyzed, studied, practiced, and mastered.

Conversation Analysis

Conversation Analysis is a broad field from the social sciences that deals with the structure of conversations. It began mostly from sociologists trying to find out what was happening in varying phone calls, and what they found was that conversation is not mostly free-form with little structure holding it together. Rather, and critical to this program, they found that conversation is a highly structured system. People base what they say on what the people before them have already said. This program teaches some of the more common patterns of our highly-structured system of conversation.

Vocabulary

Words that students most commonly have to look up have been defined for them at the beginning of each reading. I've made an attempt not to simplify the vocabulary but rather to provide realistic readings they will encounter in the academic context.

Cards

Most books on conversation have lists, sometimes lengthy lists, of phrases students should use in conversation. This program has used an abbreviated form of those lists – what I consider the most common and most useful phrases from years of testing – and has placed these phrases on cards. Each chapter then presents the phrases, and the students should use the cards with those phrases. By placing key phrases on cards and having the students play the cards as they use the phrases, students are encouraged to consciously use the phrases. It is also important that they can see what phrases and strategies they are and are not using. The cards and the explanations of how to use the cards in conversation, in pair activities and group activities, are what make this product a program rather than just a book.

Formulaic Language: The Two Levels of Conversation

Language researchers have found that more that 50% of what we say in English is formulaic phrases while the other half is more creative. The creative portion of our speaking is often difficult to acquire, involving a great deal of knowledge about grammar rules. These formulaic phrases are also difficult because they often have various social meaning that non-native speakers of English may not be aware of. Thus, it is important to know both the meanings of the phrases and how they are used in conversations. Refer to *figure 1* on the next page.

This program works with both the formulaic and the creative parts of English but specifically focuses on getting you to learn, know how to use, practice and master the most basic and essential formulaic phrases for English conversations. The phrases presented in this book are essential for success in conversation because they are used to position each individual in relation to others and the topic. These phrases enable us to successfully complete various social moves in conversation, including entering conversations, agreeing and disagreeing, expressing opinions, asking others to repeat what they've said, rephrasing an opinion, and many more. Furthermore, because we typically begin a statement with a formulaic phrase, it is essential to be able to use these phrases correctly in order to get into the conversation at all and in appropriate ways.

The creative level is important and has been the focus of most language instruction books. On the creative level, we make statements about how we perceive the world around us. Grammar and vocabulary helps students with the creative level of language; formulaic phrases helps more with the social level of language. In this book, we will concentrate on both aspects of conversations, both the formulaic and creative levels. For the creative level, you will read short passages on controversial topics and then formulate and briefly write responses to and opinions of these topics. Without preparation, it will be difficult for you to speak and practice. For the formulaic level, you will learn one or more conversation moves and expressions that go along with each move. Cards with these expressions are provided, and you will use these cards as you engage in conversation. By the end of the book, you should be adept at all conversation moves contained herein.

FIGURE 1: FORMULAIC LANGUAGE VS. CREATIVE LANGUAGE

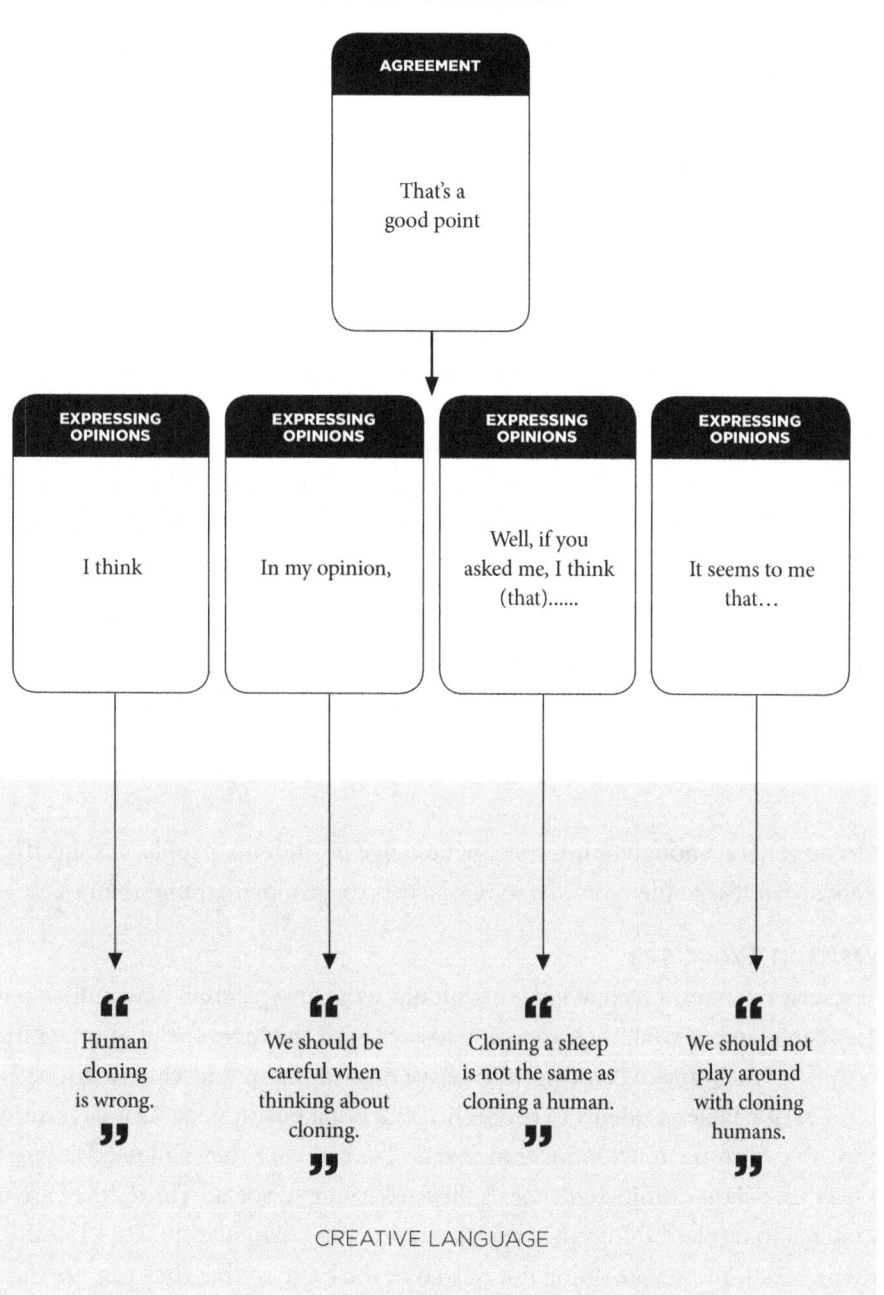

FORMULAIC LANGUAGE

AGREEMENT

That's a good point

EXPRESSING OPINIONS

I think

EXPRESSING OPINIONS

In my opinion,

EXPRESSING OPINIONS

Well, if you asked me, I think (that)......

EXPRESSING OPINIONS

It seems to me that…

" Human cloning is wrong. "

" We should be careful when thinking about cloning. "

" Cloning a sheep is not the same as cloning a human. "

" We should not play around with cloning humans. "

CREATIVE LANGUAGE

Perhaps the most important aspect to your success with the conversation game is possibly something you would not expect: laughter. Throughout the book, you will be reading a wide range of topics on various controversial topics. Some of these topics may be of interest to you. I suggest you put any strong feelings about these topics aside while using this book and rather concentrate on acquiring conversation skills. Have an open mind, or express opinions exactly opposite yours. The key is to have fun, be crazy, say crazy things, but say them! You cannot improve your English if you are too concerned about what others will think of your opinion or if you are worried about offending others. Rather, what is important is that you learn and practice new conversation skills, so I recommend you focus on improving your language skills and not on expressing your opinion or getting to the bottom of these topics.

ELEMENTS OF THE PROGRAM

This program is comprised of ten chapters, and each chapter is divided into three sections. Each chapter contains a group of phrases to learn, tied to particular adjacency pairs and conversation moves or strategies. Each of the three sections of the chapter contains a particular way, or strategy, to use the phrases (perhaps combined with already seen phrases), a new topic, a pair-work section in which students practice using the phrases and the new conversation strategy, and a group work section (The Conversation Game) in which students use the new strategies and all other strategies previously learned. The conversation games are the crux of the program and the place in which students can go from having knowledge about the viewed conversation strategies and moves to actually mastering those strategies. A scorecard has been provided in Appendix E. Students should count the number of cards they have used and record this number on the scorecard.

Formulaic Phrases

Each chapter has a group of common formulaic phrases that correspond to the conversation strategies discussed in each chapter. I have attempted to include only the most commonly used phrases. It is hoped that you not only learn these phrases but, more importantly, that you master the use of these phrases in conversation.

Topics

Topics are meant to be general enough to interest a wide range of students/people, yet specific enough to enable people to talk about them at length. The topics have been grouped around themes.

Questions & Written Exercises

After each topic is a series of questions that students should write answers to. I have students write these answers so that they can plan out what they are going to say about the topic ahead of time rather than wasting valuable class time having them try to come up with answers to topics in mid-conversation. There are several advantages to this. First, it enables students to carefully think out a position, or various positions, on the topic. Second, students are able to come up with the grammar and vocabulary they will need before the conversation, so they don't have to think about it mid-sentence as they are trying to speak. Third, there are times when it is beneficial for students to think of things they can say to practice particular moves. Thus, for example, in Chapter 5, I ask them to talk about something not related to the topic so that they can use the strategy of managing the conversation and interrupting, and in Chapter 3, I ask them to think of several ways to say something so when they are asked to rephrase what they've said, they can say the same thing in a new way. In other words, by having students complete the written portion of the program, they are better able to practice the conversation moves and strategies presented in each chapter.

Conversation Moves/Strategies

Each conversation strategy is accompanied by either a diagram of how to use the cards to carry out the strategy or a sample dialogue of how the strategy plays out in a conversation. Students should use these diagrams or dialogues as models as they engage in their pair work activities. The pair work activities are similar to guided practices—scaffolded practices of these conversation moves. After students are fairly comfortable using the strategies and moves in the pair practice they should move on to the conversation games, which provide less-scaffolded practice since they are used with the cards.

This program provides detailed instruction on a large number of conversational strategies. These strategies can be grouped into larger meta-strategies:

- **Turn-Taking:** This is the most basic conversational strategy or mechanism, and it involves various conversationalists coordinating their participation as they speak.

- **Adjacency Pairs:** Almost all strategies, except for some of the "managing discussions" strategies discussed below, are what conversation analysts call adjacency pairs. An adjacency pair is two common types of phrases or types of moves that typically come together. Examples include:

    QUESTION-ANSWER:
    A: *What time is it?*
    B: *I dunno.*

    OR GREETING-GREETING
    A: *Hello.*
    B: *Hello! Long time no see.*

Each chapter presents both units of the adjacency pair together, and thus we learn to practice both the 'A' and the 'B' parts of the unit together.

- **Managing the Discussion:** These are phrases and moves that help us to guide the topic along. If the group is getting off the topic, we can use some of these strategies to guide the group back to the original topic, or if the group is moving too slowly, we can speed the group along. Some of these are adjacency pairs, and some of them are phrases all to themselves that do not demand or need any sort of response.

- **Buying Time:** Often times we need more time to tzzzzzhink about our response, particularly if we need to generate creative language. There are several combinations of moves and strategies that allow us more time to think, and these are called 'buying time' strategies.

- **Opening up the Floor:** There are a couple of strategies that enable us to continue to speak but not say anything about the topic. These are used to try to get other participants to express their opinions about the topic.

- **Softening the Blow:** Often times, the conversational move we wish to make may be offensive to another individual – like telling them they are not speaking clearly enough, or disagreeing with them. We can make this threatening move not as threatening by adding phrases to soften the harshness of the phrase. They are called 'softening the blow' because they are intended to make the threatening moves less painful.

- **Other Moves:** There are still many other moves that we won't classify here, including reining in tangents, acknowledging and minimizing counterarguments, etc. These are more specific moves that do not branch across many adjacency pair types, and thus are treated in more detail in the chapters in which they are found.

Pair Work & Group Work (Conversation Games)

Each conversation move and strategy is first illustrated through diagrams and/or dialogues. After studying the diagrams and/or dialogues, students are directed to complete a pair work activity in which they practice that particular move or strategy only. Afterwards, they are to form groups (recommended 4-6 members) in which they practice all strategies and moves learned up to that point. The aim is to move the students from learning about a new move or strategy to using it in a guided practice (pair work) activity, and then to use it in a freer activity (group work). They should continue to practice learned strategies throughout the program, so the program is cumulative.

Variations/Drills

Drills are included in order to help you really master the conversation strategies and moves presented in the book. These drills are here to help you be able to use the strategies automatically and unconsciously when you are having a normal conversation. Keep in mind, these drills may seem unusual or odd to you because the focus in these drills is not really on communicating but rather mastering moves, using the moves in unusual ways.

Teacher's role

The role of the teacher in this program is one of more a coach than a teacher. Teachers may present each conversation strategy and move in each section of the chapter. Afterwards, the teacher may take on various roles depending on the individual needs and circumstances of the class. Here are some possibilities:

- Present and model strategies
- Check to make sure students are completing the written section of the text, check and record their scores at the end
- Take notes on what students say and give feedback on content and language
- Play along with the students to show them how to use the program
- Help students design extra practice opportunities for each chapter depending on their needs
- Discuss idiosyncrasies with some strategies depending on varying types of English

DIAGNOSTIC

Individual Work

Read the passage and answer the questions:

TOPIC #1: PUBLIC SMOKING BAN

VOCABULARY

a/the ban: – a law that does not allow certain behavior
to ban: – to make a law that does not allow certain behavior

Smoking in public has become a controversial issue in the last 15 years in the US. During this time, many states have begun to restrict the areas in which smokers may light up.

In the 1980s, for example, people could smoke on airplanes, but in 1989, the government made a law that prohibits smoking on all domestic flights. They reasoned that people share a small space on an airplane, and smoke would have to be breathed in by everyone on that plane.

Later, states and cities began regulating the public areas in which smoking was permitted. In California, for example, smoking is only permitted in the privacy of your home. You may not smoke on the street, in a bar, in a restaurant, or anywhere. In September of 2005, a similar smoking ban came into effect in Austin, Texas. Now, people may smoke on the street, but they may not smoke in restaurants, bars, or nightclubs.

The main rationale for limiting public smoking is the fact that second hand smoke, smoke breathed out by the smoker, is often breathed in by non-smokers. Some have even gone so far as to say that second hand smoke is deadlier than first hand smoke because non-smokers breathe in the smoke without any filter. Thus, to protect people's right to breathe clean air, cities and states have created smoking bans.

Many smokers are not happy about this situation. They feel they have been forced to smoke in small, uncomfortable areas, often a small space outside of their workplace or school. Also, in cities that have banned smoking in all buildings, bars, and night clubs, the owners of these businesses claim that smoking bans cause fewer people to go out and spend money, which negatively impacts their businesses.

1 What do you think about smoking bans?

2 In what places, if any, should smoking be prohibited?

3 Is it fair to place smokers into certain areas where they must smoke?

4 Is it fair for non-smokers to have to breathe in second hand smoke? Is second hand smoke really as dangerous as some claim it to be?

5 Should economics (how much money restaurant and bar owners make) influence our decision on banning smoking?

PAIR WORK

Find a partner and briefly discuss the questions related to this topic. This is designed to be a warm-up to a group discussion. Talk for approximately five minutes.

GROUP WORK

Form groups of 4-6 people. Discuss public smoking bans. Use some sort of recording device to record your conversation. You may wish to have one recording and then share this electronically (through email, upload Wto a class website, etc.), or each individual may have his or her own recording device.

WRITTEN ASSIGNMENT: DIAGNOSTIC

Listen to and transcribe your conversation. Try to transcribe exactly what you've said, including any grammar or wording mistakes, pronunciation mistakes, long pauses, hesitations, and repetitions. After you've transcribed it, have your teacher help you find all wording and grammar mistakes. For a simple diagnostic, you can count the following:

	Diagnostic
Number of turns:	
Number of words per turn:	
Number of mistakes:	
Mistakes/total words:	
Mistakes/number of turns:	

At the end of the course, you will complete another test to see your progress.

BASIC SKILLS FOR CONVERSATIONS

OBJECTIVES OF THIS CHAPTER
- Introduce students to conversation games
- Introduce students to expressing opinions
- Introduce students to agreeing
- Introduce students to disagreeing

This chapter presents the foundation for conversation skills in English. First, you will learn to express your opinion. Next, you will learn to agree and disagree with the opinions of others. Finally, you will learn to combine agreement/disagreement with expressing your own opinion.

EXPRESSING OPINIONS, AGREEING AND DISAGREEING

The first conversation moves that you will learn are the most basic: expressing your opinion, agreeing and disagreeing. In English, we have various expressions for expressing our opinion, such as *in my opinion, I think (that), I feel (that), it seems to me (that), my sense is (that).* You will begin with these five expressions. Following each expression, you will state something of substance at the meaning level, such as "*I think (that)* school uniforms are great," or "*My sense is that* school uniforms are of absolutely no use to students in the modern world." Once you have stated your opinion, your partner will agree or disagree with you using an agreement or disagreement card.

To practice, read the following passage on learning a language. Then, answer the questions that follow.

Expressions

Expressing your opinion
In my opinion, …
I think (that) …
I feel (that) …
My sense is (that) …
It seems to me (that) …
I can't help thinking that …

Agreement
I feel the same way.
I agree.
You're right.
Right.
That's a good point
I've never thought of it that way.
Exactly.
Good point.
I couldn't agree with you more.

Disagreement
I hate to disagree with you, but don't you think …
I'm sorry, but I disagree.
I disagree.
I'm not so sure about that.
Yes, but don't you think …
I see your point, but don't you think …

TURN-TAKING USING BASIC EXPRESSIONS

English conversation is similar to soccer or basketball: one individual speaks for a while and then passes the turn to another individual, who speaks for a while, and then passes the turn to someone else. In this first chapter, we will learn how to pass the turn from person to person using the *opinion, agreement,* and *disagreement* expressions.

TOPIC #2: LEARNING A LANGUAGE

Read the passage and answer the questions. Write about both sides of the argument. The more you write, the better prepared for speaking you will be.

VOCABULARY
consistently – *always*
varying degrees of – *different quantities or amounts or intensities of something*

In today's world, it is common and important to have learned at least one foreign language. Those who have learned a foreign language typically have a good idea what works for them and what doesn't work. However, experts, those who study language learning, often have strong opinions on the best ways to learn a language.

Many teachers these days believe that what is needed is for students to read and listen to lots of language. They believe that the more language reading and listening students do, the better they will be when they attempt to speak and write it. These teachers and experts often argue that students should never be forced to write or speak.

Some teachers and scholars believe that teachers should never correct students when they make errors. They believe that correcting errors only causes students to avoid speaking or writing or at least to avoid difficult language structures. For example, if a teacher corrects a student's use of the irregular past tense, the student will avoid using the past tense altogether. However, others point out that if students are consistently corrected on all grammar errors, and students were to avoid their errors, then they would be unable to speak at all. Furthermore, many students expect teachers to correct them.

For vocabulary, many believe that memorization is a waste of time. Rather, students should "naturally acquire" language by hearing words in context. Definitions, dictionaries, and memorization are of no use and simply a waste of time. Others feel that varying degrees of memorization is beneficial, especially to the adult learner.

1 What is your opinion on this topic?

2 How do your ways of studying a language compare with those of the experts?

3 Do you prefer your teacher to correct you when you make a mistake? Why or why not?

4 Should students ever be forced to produce language? Why or why not?

5 What is the best way to learn vocabulary? Why?

6 Are there any other ways that you have found beneficial in your own learning experience? What are they?

Preparation for Practice with Expressions

Get out your cards and remove the *opinion, agreement*, and *disagreement* cards. Read through the cards and the expressions on the cards. Lay your cards out on your table, desk, or floor—wherever you are going to play.

EXAMPLE OF PLACEMENT OF CARDS

PAIR WORK

Find a partner you can work with. Work only on question one—"Do you think that the world should have a common language?" If so, what language should it be? Partner A should express an opinion, and partner B can agree or disagree with that opinion, and then express an opinion. Partner A can then respond with an agreement or disagreement card. Each time you express an opinion, agree, or disagree, use a card with an expression on it. The point of this exercise.is to master correct conversational expressions, not to really discuss these topics. Use as many cards as you can in a limited time.

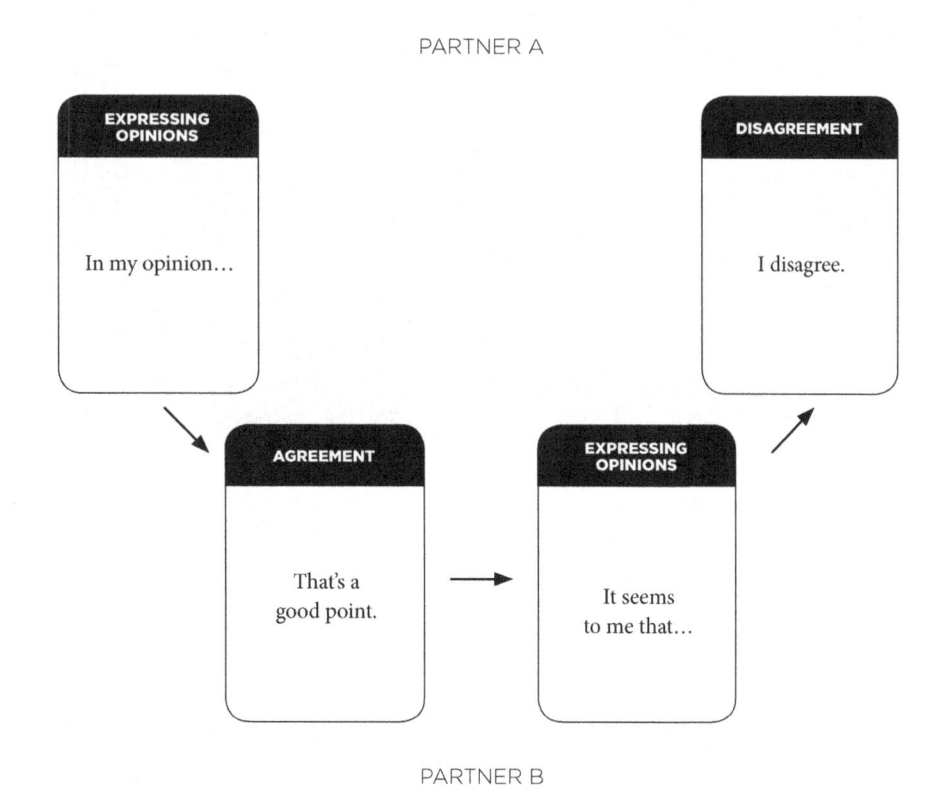

PARTNER A

PARTNER B

THE CONVERSATION GAME 15

CONVERSATION GAME

Divide into groups of 3-6. Discuss the preceding topic. Discuss and answer all questions. Use a card every time you speak. You should be able to use a minimum of 10 cards in 15 minutes. Record the number of cards played. Sort them by color and record their numbers on a scorecard (Appendix E).

Assess yourself by asking how you did. If you used all of your cards, you are phenomenal and ready for the next step. If you used less than three of any single card, you need to increase the number of those cards in subsequent games. Give yourself a goal for the next game, such as:

1 Use a minimum of three agreement/disagreement/opinion cards.

2 Use more than 12 cards total.

3 Use all agreement/disagreement/opinion cards.

Opening Up the Floor with Agreement

A common *strategy* that happens in English conversation is to open up the floor. Opening up the floor means providing anyone the opportunity to speak. In some languages this is done simply through silence, but in English, we avoid long periods of silence by using filler phrases – phrases that have little creative content but say something socially. In this case, the filler phrases say that anyone can speak. The first filler phrase we can use is an agreement phrase. After having agreed with someone else's opinion, if no one else takes the turn to express an opinion, we can continue to use agreement fillers until someone decides to express an opinion.

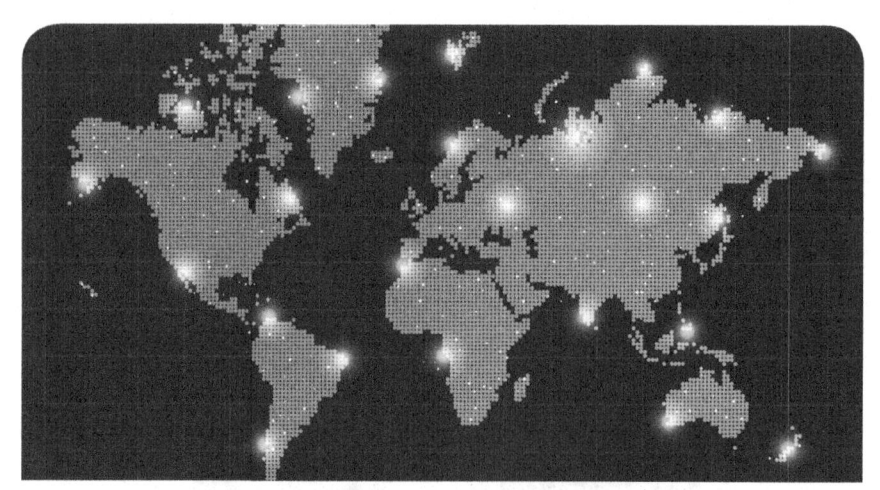

TOPIC #3: WORLD LANGUAGE

Read the passage below and answer the questions.

VOCABULARY

expand - to get bigger
conduct business - do business
force someone to do something - make someone do something, probably something that they do not want to do
translate - to rewrite in a different language
tongue - language

Currently, the world does not have a common language. However, long periods of peace have typically been accompanied by a common language. When the Roman Empire expanded, many people in that area of the world learned to speak Latin or Greek, and the use of these common languages enabled people to conduct business more easily. Today, we are faced with the possibility of having a worldwide common language, and many have debated what language this should be.

There are several obvious advantages to having a common language. Were we to all speak the same language, we could communicate with people from other cultures more easily, and thus perhaps reduce conflicts. Similarly, if works of literature were translated into a common language, anyone who understood the common language could access works of literature from around the globe.

Another obvious advantage to having a common language is the ability of people to travel and study in foreign countries. Currently, most academic work is done in English. Most international journals are published in English, and many universities, even outside of English speaking countries, conduct course work in English, so having a common language has definitely enabled people from around the globe to study diverse subjects ranging from mathematics, science, and engineering to music, art, and literature.

However, there are also many arguments against having a common tongue. Perhaps the most convincing argument to not having a common tongue is the fact that many languages would be lost as people would begin communicating only in the common tongue and leaving the language of their region or country behind. In fact, over the last few hundred years, thousands of languages have already disappeared, and this alarming trend is expected to continue. Scholars who study language have pointed to the great loss in human knowledge: different languages may function completely differently, and we could learn a great deal by studying many of these small languages, but once the languages are dead (not spoken by anyone anymore), they can no longer be studied, at least in their spoken forms.

Others have argued that one's identity is deeply tied to one's language. By forcing everyone to speak the same language, we would lose a great deal of diversity. And importantly, works of literature lose much of their meaning when translated into a foreign tongue. This is particularly an issue with religious texts. Many Christians spend a great deal of effort learning the languages that the Bible was written in in order to better understand it. The holy book of Muslims, the Quran, should not be translated but rather read only in its original form.

Finally, choosing one language over all others would unfairly favor one culture group or groups over others. Thus, for example, selecting English would favor the UK, the US and other English speaking countries over all non-English speaking countries.

1 Do you think that the world should have a common language? If so, what language should it be?

2 Would a common language help international commerce? Do you see any disadvantages to having a common language for the business world?

3 Would having a common language help to resolve or limit cultural conflicts between people? Would we have fewer wars?

4 Would it be beneficial for all literature to be translated into a common language? Should literature be kept in its original language? Why/why not?

5 Does selecting one language as a common language (e.g. English) unfairly favor people from countries who speak that language? If so, is this a reason not to have a common language? In other words, should we avoid creating a common language in order not to favor particular countries?

PAIR WORK

Find a partner you can work with. Work only on question one – should the world have a common language? Practice using your cards as you did with the previous conversation, but this time, try to use multiple agreement cards at the same time. The point of this exercise is to master the use of culturally appropriate ways of speaking – using several agreement expressions together to avoid expressing an opinion and to open up the floor to other speakers.

Conversation Move #2: Using Agreement to Open Up the Floor

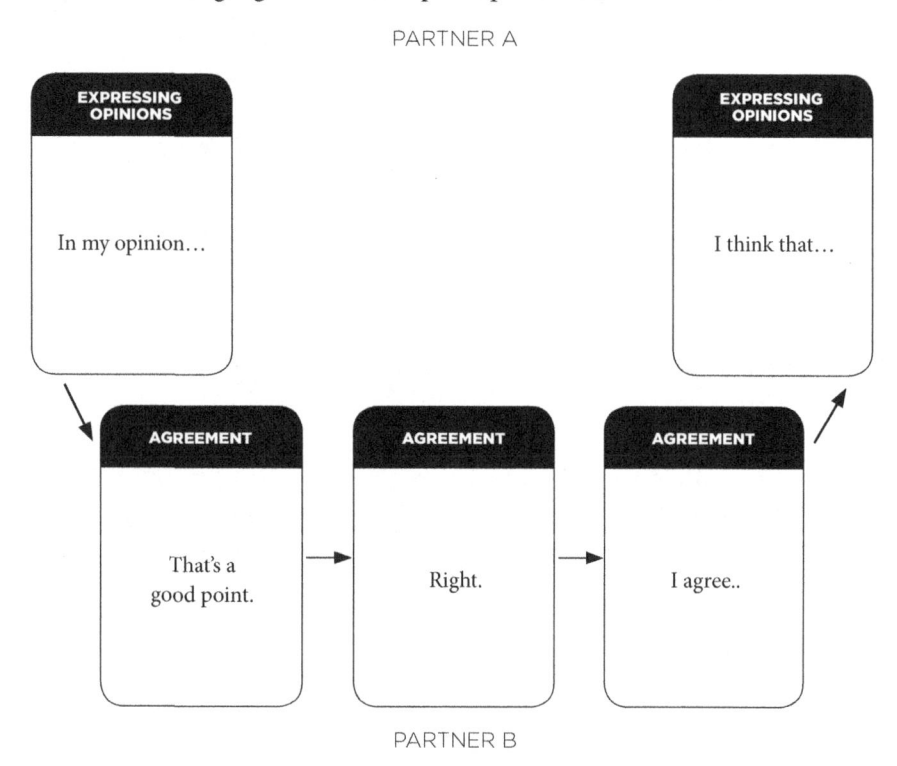

PARTNER A

EXPRESSING OPINIONS				EXPRESSING OPINIONS
In my opinion…				I think that…

AGREEMENT	AGREEMENT	AGREEMENT
That's a good point.	Right.	I agree..

PARTNER B

CONVERSATION GAME

Divide into groups of 3-6. Discuss the preceding topic. Attempt to use as many agreement cards as you can. Record the number of cards played. Sort them by color and record their numbers in the chart below.

Conversation Strategy: Buying Time with "In + I"

Another conversational strategy is to buy time, which is to use expressions that have no significant creative meaning but allow you more time to think of a response. These are useful when you are trying to think of the next word or grammar structure. In this first buying time strategy, you will use the phrase "In my opinion" plus another opinion expression that begins with 'I.'

TOPIC #4: STANDARDIZED ENGLISH TESTS

Read the passage below and answer the questions.

VOCABULARY

standardized Tests – *tests that measure students' ability. These include the TOEFL, the SAT, the GRE, the TOEIC, IELTS, etc. We usually use "the" before the acronym (capital letters like "SAT") before the test.*
particular – *specific or unique.*
particularly – *especially*
complaint – *expressing unhappiness*
partial consideration – *one part of many parts that are looked at*
well-constructed – *built or made in a good way.*
claim – *argue, but perhaps without strong or conclusive (definitive) evidence*
accurately – *precise or without error*
unable – *not able*
cheat/cheating – *to break rules to do better on the test*
occur – *happen*
admit to school – *get into school, get accepted to school*
lack – *not have*
effectively/effective – *done in a successful way*

Standardized tests are often employed to measure students' ability in a particular area. These tests are usually used as a partial consideration for entrance to the university. Many books and other materials are sold to students trying to pass these standardized tests. ESL students are particularly interested in these tests because they must obtain good scores on these tests to be get into universities.

A common complaint of ESL teachers is that students want to study for these tests, but they do not want to learn English. Thus, students may not want to do what teachers assign them to do and rather choose to study for a test. Teachers accuse students of not being interested in learning how to have a conversation, how to use idioms and slang, or how to pronounce a word correctly, but students claim that success in these tests is what is most important because it determines their future. Students are more interested in getting into school, graduating, and obtaining a good job, while some teachers want students to learn more about culture or interesting aspects of English.

However, some argue that a well-constructed test should always test a wide range of skills and can test one's general ability. Thus, studying for a test is helpful for improving one's general English ability, and there is no difference between test English and regular, everyday English.

There are other complaints about standardized English tests as well. Some schools claim that these tests do not accurately measure a person's language ability. They find that students may be able to get high scores on the test but unable to write and speak in English. There are also stories of cheating, especially where a student will hire a professional test taker to take the test for him or her.

1 What is your opinion of standardized English tests?

2 Do you think these tests accurately measure a student's English ability?

3 Is "real English" different from "test English"?

4 Do students need more than "test English" to do well in school?

5 Do you think cheating occurs on standardized tests? Is it a big problem?

6 What should universities do when a student is admitted based on his or her standardized test score (such as the TOEFL or TOIEC) but lacks the ability to communicate effectively with others?

....

....

....

PAIR WORK

Find a partner you can work with. Work only on question one – what is your opinion on standardized tests? Practice using your cards as you did with the previous conversation, but this time, apply the strategy below of using "In my opinion" + "I think/I feel/I can't help thinking …" The use of these two cards together gives you extra time to think of how you're going to word your opinion. We can call this the In + I buying for time strategy. Note, you cannot just use any two opinion expressions together.

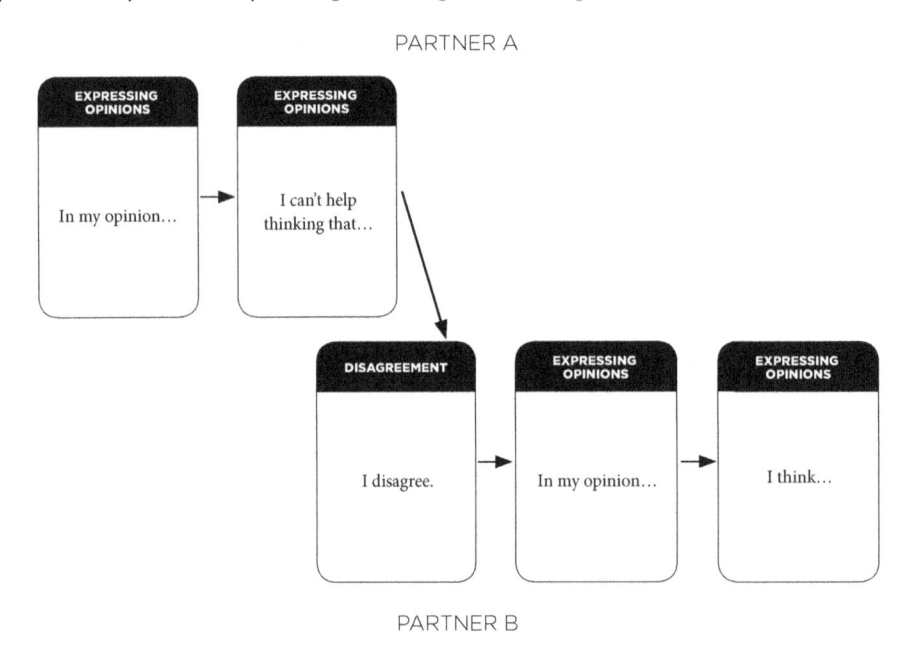

PARTNER A

EXPRESSING OPINIONS	EXPRESSING OPINIONS
In my opinion…	I can't help thinking that…

DISAGREEMENT	EXPRESSING OPINIONS	EXPRESSING OPINIONS
I disagree.	In my opinion…	I think…

PARTNER B

CONVERSATION GAME

Divide into groups of 3-6. Discuss the preceding topic. Attempt to discuss and answer all questions. Use as many cards as you can. Record the number of cards played. Sort them by color and record their numbers on a scorecord (Appendix E).

LEADING A CONVERSATION

OBJECTIVES OF THIS CHAPTER
- Introduce and lead a conversation
- Move individuals through questions using correct expressions
- Summarize a topic and/or a discussion, to summarize what others have said
- Conclude a discussion

In the last chapter you learned how to express your opinion and how to agree and disagree with others. In this chapter, you will learn how to lead a conversation using more formulaic expressions. These expressions will help you introduce and conclude a conversation, move a conversation along, and summarize a discussion. The expressions you will learn in this chapter will also be useful in other situations including wrapping up presentations, classes, or other formal speaking situations.

In the first round, you will learn how to begin a conversation. You will learn four phrases that you can use, in order, without adding anything except the name of the topic. You never have to vary this formula for introducing a topic, although may want to make a few modifications to it as you become more familiar with leading.

In the second round, you will learn how to conclude a conversation. This is more difficult and involves some turn-taking with other participants as well as creating a summary of the group's discussion. In the final round, you'll learn a simple phrase that will enable you to introduce new questions. This phrase can be modified to be used in a wide range of situations, not just academic scenarios.

Because you will not always be leading a conversation, you will want to bookmark this chapter and return to it when it is your turn to lead again.

Expressions

Introduction
Our topic today is …
I'd like to know what you think about …
What's your opinion on this topic?
Would anyone like to comment?

Conclusion
I'd like to summarize our discussions so far.
Let's wind up our conversation, I'll take one more comment.
I'm sorry, our time is up.
Thank you for your participation.

Keeping the Conversation Moving
Let's move on to the next/last question.

Role of the Leader

The main role of the leader in a conversation is to manage the topic and the participants. It is important to properly introduce and conclude the topic, and it is also important to make sure that equal time is spent on each question. Leaders should look at the total time for the discussion and spend an appropriate amount on each question. If the group spends too much time on the questions, then it won't finish the topic, and if the group moves too quickly through the questions, it will finish the topic too soon. Thus, the leader must try to move the group through the questions at an appropriate speed.

The secondary role of the leader is to participate as a participant. This means expressing opinion, agreeing and disagreeing with others, and using any of the strategies and expressions that you'll see in the later chapters. As a leader, we need to make sure that we are using all of the leader expressions, but we can also use the regular expressions as well.

Introducing a Topic

We do not need to be creative when introducing a topic. Rather, we simply need to say the expressions on the first four introduction cards, in order. Thus, at the beginning of a conversation, our focus should be on making eye contact with group members and making them feel comfortable to speak and not on trying to produce creative language.

TOPIC #5: ASTROLOGY

Read the passage below and answer the questions.

VOCABULARY

happenings - things that happen
ties A to B - connects A to B.
superstition - a belief that has little scientific proof, so many think it is a myth
to be termed - to be called
to affect (v) - influence
to support their position - to give facts and evidence to make their argument stronger
evidence - facts, stories, numbers, or any kind of data that can be used to support an argument
to be attributed to - to say one thing caused something
directly overhead - exactly above
infamous - famous for being bad
disprove - show (prove) that something is not true

Astrology is the study of how objects in the sky, such as stars and planets, influence happenings on the earth. Astrology is an old science, and until about the 1700s, it was the only way humans studied stars and planets. However, astrology always ties the movement of objects in the sky to happenings on Earth. In the 1700s, scientists in the Enlightenment saw astrology as superstition and began studying the movement of planets and stars with no reference to occurrences on the earth. This new science was termed Astronomy.

Astronomers and other scientists believe astrology to be a superstition and not a real science. They claim that there have been no studies that show how movement in the stars affects things on earth. Astrologers disagree, and they claim that research is difficult to do. They have provided some research to support their position.

One piece of evidence that astrologers give to support their point of view is the fact that there are some trends in human characteristics that can be attributed to the position of planets and the stars. The Mars effect is one. Basically, when the planet Mars is directly overhead when a child is born, he or she has a much greater chance of becoming an athletic super star than do others. Also, many famous or infamous people were born when there was a unique alignment of the planets. Examples include Bill Clinton, Hillary Clinton, Napoleon and Hitler.

1 What is your opinion of astrology?

2 Do you think that astrology is superstition? Do you believe in astrology?

3 Do you believe in the Mars effect or in other similar such effects?

4 Is there astrology in your country? Is it similar to or different from Western astrology?

5 Do you know your Zodiac sign? Do you think that you fit the description of this sign or not?

6 Have you had any other experiences that would prove or disprove astrology?

....

....

....

Preparation for Leaders

Introduction and conclusion cards are always said in order, so you do not need to choose which card to use, just use the next one in order. The order is given at the beginning of this chapter. The leader should also always use all leader cards. There is never a reason not to use all the leader cards.

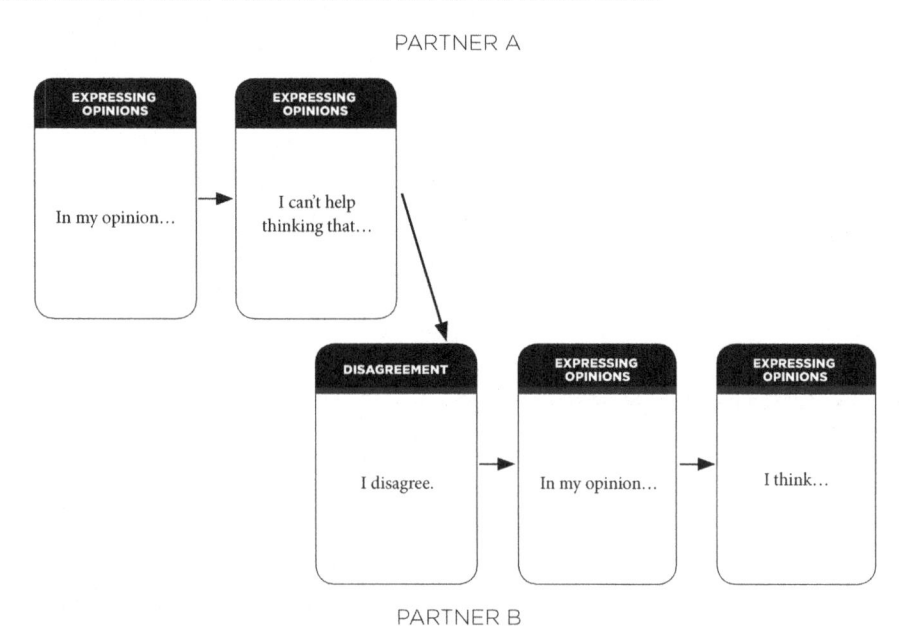

PARTNER A

[EXPRESSING OPINIONS: "In my opinion…"] → [EXPRESSING OPINIONS: "I can't help thinking that…"]
↓
[DISAGREEMENT: "I disagree."] → [EXPRESSING OPINIONS: "In my opinion…"] → [EXPRESSING OPINIONS: "I think…"]

PARTNER B

CONVERSATION GAME

Divide into groups of 3-6. Discuss the preceding topic. Attempt to discuss and answer all questions. Use as many cards as you can. Record the number of cards played. Sort them by color and record their numbers on a scorecard (Appendix E).

PAIR WORK

Find a partner, and practice introducing all of the four topics you've read so far. Follow the script below *exactly*. You do not need to vary from this script. Partner A can introduce topic #1, and then partner B can introduce topic #1. Then, move on to topics 2, 3, and 4.

Sample Dialogue #1: Topic: Learning a Language

A: **Our topic today** is learning a language

A: **I'd like to know what you think about** learning a language.

A: **What's your opinion on this topic?**

A: **Would anyone like to comment?**

B: **In my opinion, I think** that learning a language is really difficult, and that each person has his or her own way to learn a language.

(A and B switch roles)

Sample Dialogue—Topic: Standardized tests

B: **Our topic today** is standardized tests.

B: **I'd like to know what you think about** standardized tests.

B: **What's your opinion on this topic?**

B: **Would anyone like to comment?**

A: Well, I personally hate taking standardized tests, but I also think they are necessary.

CONVERSATION GAME

Divide into groups of 3-6. Choose one person as the leader. The leader may choose to use only leader cards or use leader cards and the cards presented in chapter 1. Discuss the preceding topic. Attempt to discuss and answer all questions. Use as many cards as you can. Sort cards by color and record your score on a scorecard (Appendix E).

Moving the Discussion along

At times, it will be necessary to move from one question to the next in the conversation. When taking on the role of leader, we need to make sure we cover all questions and that we allocate an approximately equal amount of time to each question. We can smoothly introduce a new question using the phrases in this chapter.

TOPIC #6: FENG SHUI

Read the passage below and answer the questions.

VOCABULARY

spatially - Their arrangement in space
living spaces - where they live
consult - ask for adviceW
rearrange - change the placement of
doubtful - something that is probably not true
anecdote - a personal story used to prove a point

In Chinese, feng means wind, and shui means water. According to the Chinese, water and wind will help people to live better if they are spatially arranged well. Feng shui is considered both an art and a science, and people study and follow it in order to improve various parts of their lives including relationships, love lives, knowledge, and money. Many people make decisions on their living spaces based on feng shui.

For example, one money manager was told to always keep the lid down in the toilet in her office. The toilet is located in the direction in which money is important. According to feng shui, if the toilet seat is up, then money will flow into and out of the toilet through the pipes. Also, Donald Trump, a prominent US real estate business man, is said to never make any decision without first consulting a feng shui expert.

Feng shui specialists often advise people to place their beds in a certain direction so that they will sleep better, or to place an aquarium next to the front door in order to make more money. They also advise sitting so that your back is not to the door or placing large mirrors in bedrooms. But some of these ideas seem to be simply common sense and having nothing to do with the science of feng shui. For example, if you sit with your back to the door of your office, you cannot see when someone enters, so they can come in and surprise you, and similarly, if you have a large mirror in your room, you might wake up to your reflection, which might not be exactly what you want to see early in the morning.

In the last couple of decades, feng shui has become popular in the US. Many books are available to help people follow the ideas of this Eastern science, and some people believe they have benefited greatly by rearranging their living spaces. Others, however, are more doubtful. They see feng shui as a superstition and not a science. They consider it a waste of time and money. In their defense, there have not been many empirical studies as to the effect of arranging living spaces in particular ways. Rather, the benefits of this ancient science come mostly from anecdotes, or people's personal stories.

1 What do you think about *feng shui*? Is it a myth, or is it real?

2 Do you believe that *feng shui* can make you healthier, or richer, or more successful in parts of your life?

3 Is *feng shui* common or popular in your country?

4 Do you follow any ideas put forward by *feng shui*? Why or why not?

5 Putting *feng shui* aside for a moment, do you think there are benefits to arranging one's living space in a neat or particular fashion? Can you give examples from your own experience?

PAIR WORK

Find a partner and practice very briefly discussing any topic seen thus far. Partner A should use the phrases to introduce the topic, and partner B should answer the questions in 20 seconds or less. Partner A should use the phrase "Let's move on to the next/last question." Then, choose another topic and switch roles.

Sample Dialogue

A: **_Our topic today is_** astrology.

A: **_I'd like to know what you think about_** astrology.

A: **_What's your opinion on this topic_**?

A: **_Would anyone like to comment_**?

B: **_In my opinion, I think_** that astrology is very interesting, but I'm not sure whether it's accurate or not.

A: **_Let's move on to the next question_**. Do you think that astrology is superstition? Do you believe in astrology?

B: Well, I'm not sure. **_I feel_** it might be more superstition than science, but…

A: **_Let's move on to the next question_**. Do you believe in the Mars effect or in other similar such effects?

B: **_It seems to me that_** the Mars effect is bogus even though there is some evidence to back this idea up.

A: **_Let's move on to the next question_**. Is there astrology in your country? Is it similar to or different from Western astrology?

B: Yes, there is. **_I think that_** there is one different type of astrology in my country; it's Eastern or Chinese astrology. Chinese astrology is different because …

A: **_Let's move on to the next question_**. Do you know your Zodiac sign? Do you think that you fit the description of this sign or not?

B: My sign is Leo, but, **_in my opinion, it seems to me_** at least that this description doesn't completely fit my personality. For example …

A: **_Let's move on to the last question_**. Have you had any other experiences that would prove or disprove astrology?

B: **_In my opinion_**, the experiences that I have had can neither prove nor disprove astrology.

(A and B switch roles.)

CONVERSATION GAME

Divide into groups of 3-6. Discuss the preceding topic. Choose one person as your leader. The leader may use only leader cards or may use all cards thus presented. Attempt to discuss and answer all questions. Use as many cards as you can. At the end of the discussion, record your score on a scoredard (Appendix E).

Concluding Conversations

We typically use very formulaic, unchanging phrases to conclude a conversation, similar to the way we begin a conversation. This program provides four basic phrases that can be used to conclude a conversation, and they are always said in the same order, just like the introduction phrases always come in the same order. Keep these cards in order and ready for when you are leading a conversation. Concluding a conversation is a little more involved than introducing a topic because it requires the leader to summarize the conversation and also allow for final comments. For the purposes of this program, we will allow for only one more final comment at the end.

TOPIC #7: DREAMS

Read the passage below and answer the questions.

VOCABULARY

rapid-eye-movement - a period of sleep during which a person's eyes move a lot, and the person dreams
absurd - not based on what would happen in the real world
rigid - unchanging, following very predictable patterns
conscious/consciousness - a state of being fully aware of what is going on around you. This occurs when you are awake.
unconscious/unconsciousness - a state of being not aware of what is going on around you, typically when you are asleep
subconscious - what you are not typically aware of even though you are awake
shed - to take off, to lose
the core - the central part of

> The average human sleeps between seven and eight hours per night and goes through various stages of sleep. Each stage is a different level of unconsciousness. One stage is a shallow stage of sleep, characterized by rapid-eye-movement, or REM. Dreaming occurs during REM. People may not remember their dreams, but sleep scientists tell us that everyone dreams every night.

Dreams can be fantastic and absurd or boring; they may contain elements of reality or fantasy. Many people believe that dreams have no meaning and are merely entertaining. However, many believe that dreams are our connection to our unconscious minds. Those who see dreams in this way claim that brain structures become less rigid, psychological defenses relax, and individuals can experience their unconscious thoughts more clearly. This is important because, as scientists have discovered, 95% or so of our thoughts occurs below the conscious level.

Some believe that dreams can be used to predict the future. For example, one individual claims to have dreamed about the explosion of the space shuttle Columbia in 1984 the night before it happened. Others insist that they have been able to predict other world events such as the bombing of the World Trade Center.

Dreams have also been said to mark particular changes individuals go through in life. The Maya, an Indian group in Mexico and Guatemala that has a long history and has built great civilizations, believe that in the afterlife, we have to shed portions of our identity. During life, we have built particular aspects of our personality in order to get along with other human beings. However, these must be shed so that we get to the core of our identity. This is a difficult and stressful process. If a person dreams that he or she dies in a dream, that person has shed a portion of his or her false identity during life, thus making the afterlife easier. Thus, for the Maya, a dream in which one dies signals a change a person has made in his or her life.

1 What do you think about dreams?

2 Do dreams give us access to our unconscious minds? If so, is this beneficial? Why?

THE CONVERSATION GAME

3 Do dreams have any meaning, and if so, what?

4 Do dreams signal changes made in one's life? Have you ever had a dream that signaled some sort of change?

5 Can dreams be used to predict the future? Have you ever dreamt something that later came true?

PAIR WORK

Find a partner and practice very briefly discussing any topic seen thus far. Partner A should use the phrases to introduce the topic, and partner B should answer the questions in 20 seconds or less. Partner A should use the phrase "Let's move on to the next/last question". Then, choose another topic and switch roles.
(A and B switch roles.)

Note: In actual conversation games, we should be spending approximately five minutes (or more) discussing each question. Here, we are simply trying to practice using the correct phrases for moving from one question to the next.

CONVERSATION GAME

Divide into groups of 3-6. Discuss the preceding topic. Choose one person as your leader. The leader may use only leader cards or may use all cards thus presented. Attempt to discuss and answer `all questions. Use as many cards as you can. Record your score on a scorecard (Appendix E).

ASKING FOR REPETITION AND REPHRASING

OBJECTIVES OF THIS CHAPTER
- Repeat and ask for repetition
- Rephrase statements
- Practice basic conversation skills of opinions, agreement and disagreement
- Practice basic leader skills of introducing and concluding a topic, and moving through questions

When people don't understand us, we are often called upon to rephrase what we've said. In other words, we are asked to say things in a different way. Also, when we don't understand what our conversation partner has said, we may need to ask him or her to repeat as well. While individuals learning English may often get by with the simple "sorry," the material in this chapter will provide you with more sophisticated and culturally appropriate ways of asking others to repeat what they've said.

ASKING FOR REPETITION AND REPHRASING

Two common skills in any conversation situation are those of asking speakers to repeat what they've said and rephrasing what you have already said. These skills can be used in a wide range of speaking situations from sales phone calls to casual conversations to job interviews to formal presentations. In all of these situations, one speaker may ask another to rephrase him/herself, thus requiring others to repeat what they have said using different words. This skill is particularly useful for non-native speakers of English, who may have greater difficulty in producing spoken English, and may thus be asked to repeat utterances due to misunderstandings from pronunciation, word choice, or other errors native speakers avoid. Asking for repetition is also essential for non-native speakers as they have greater difficulty understanding spoken English. Luckily, there are a handful of formulaic phrases we employ to both ask for repetition and rephrase what we've said.

THE CONVERSATION GAME

Expressions

Asking for repetition

Could you speak a little more loudly?
Could you speak a little more slowly?
(I'm sorry,) I don't quite follow you.
I'm afraid I'm not clear on what you meant by that.

Rephrasing

Let me put it this way …
Basically, what I'm trying to say is …
Basically, what I'm saying is …

Turn-Taking with Asking for Repetition and Rephrasing

In Chapter 2, we learned about turn-taking with *opinion, agreement,* and *disagreement* expressions. Turn-taking works in a similar manner with *asking for repetition* and *rephrasing* expressions.

TOPIC #8: THE GROWING PROBLEM OF OBESITY

Read the passage below and answer the questions. Write between one and three sentences for each question. When you rephrase you will need to answer each question again using different words. By writing your answers ahead of time, you will create new ways of saying the same thing.

VOCABULARY

threefold: three times
overweight: weighing more than normal or healthy
obese: very overweight
rural: an area in the countryside, away from towns or cities
urban: an area in the city
radical: dramatic, extreme
advent of the TV: invention and widespread use of the TV
spare time: free time
dietary: related to diet, what you eat

Obesity, or the condition of being very overweight, is a growing global problem. While this problem began in the US, it has begun to affect most countries in the world, so the importance of this problem should not be understated: the problem of obesity is increasing in most countries of the world.

Medical experts have divided people into four different groups based on their weight, including people who are underweight, those who have an appropriate weight, those who are overweight, and those who are more than overweight, or obese. Worldwide, there are one billion people who are overweight and 300 million who are obese. In 2010 in the US alone, 63% of all adults were overweight or obese. But obesity is not limited to the US. In Europe, for example, 45% of all people are overweight, and in China, the number of overweight individuals increased threefold from 1989-1997, a period of less than ten years. The problem of obesity is affecting other countries as well.

There are two main causes of obesity. First, there has been a radical change in lifestyle over the last 50 years as people move from rural areas to the cities. Life in the countryside has typically involved more physical activity: walking to and from school or work and physical labor in rural workplaces such as farms and ranches. In the city, however, people take cars or public transportation to work, so walking is limited, and work frequently involves sitting behind a desk and working on a computer rather than physical movement. Another aspect of this phenomenon has been the change in use of spare time. In the past, people read or did outdoor activities like sports, but since the advent of the TV, people have become more accustomed to sitting in front of the TV. Now, with computer games so popular, people spend even less time doing physical activity.

The second main cause of obesity is a change in diet. Obese individuals are less likely to eat vegetables than those of normal body weight. In addition, people nowadays are more likely to eat outside the home in restaurants and at food stands. The food in these places is almost invariably less healthy than food prepared at home. In the past, food was expensive and people had little money, so they often ate at home. When they went to work, they would take food that had been prepared at home. Nowadays, most people eat lunch in restaurants. We have lots of food courts and fast food restaurants that are much more convenient than eating at home.

To conclude, obesity is a growing problem that is affecting most nations in the world. People now spend more money on health care than in the past due to the health problems that come with being overweight. In addition, the changes in lifestyle and diet, the main two causes, are now ingrained in the global culture and may be hard to change.

1 What is your opinion on this topic?

2 Is obesity a problem in your country? How long has it been a problem? Is it an increasing problem?

3 One main cause of obesity is the change from a rural to an urban lifestyle. Has this affected you or your family?

4 What do you think can be done about the change in going from a rural to an urban lifestyle?

5 What do you think can be done about the problem of dietary changes?

6 What do you think will happen in the future? In your country? In the United States? In the world?

PAIR WORK

Work with a partner to discuss the above topic. Use only opinion, rephrasing and asking for repetition cards. Try to use as many as possible. It doesn't matter if you really understand what your partner is saying. Ask him or her to rephrase it as much as possible. Also use your set of basic cards (opinion, agree, and disagree). Continue to ask each other to repeat what you've said until each partner has used a minimum of five asking for repetition cards and eight rephrasing cards.

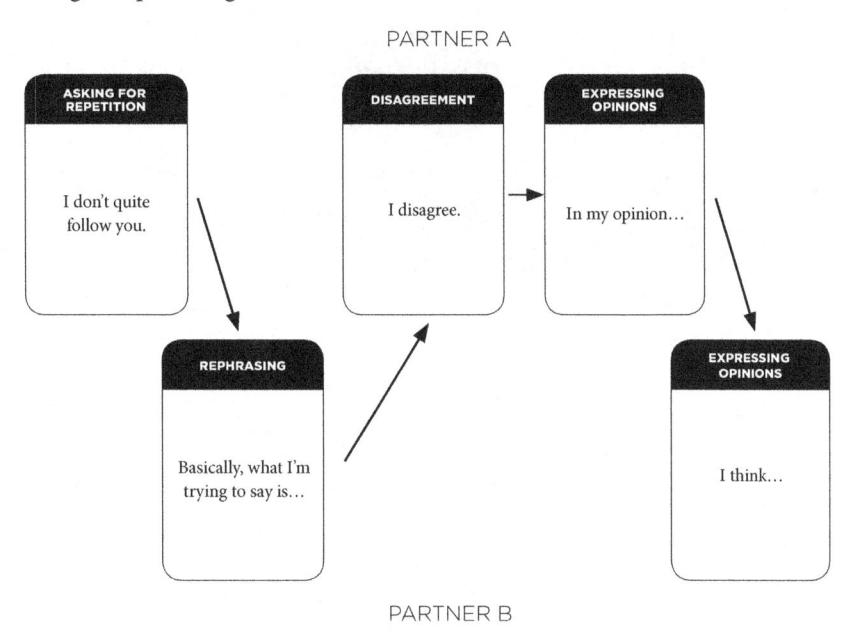

PARTNER A

- ASKING FOR REPETITION: I don't quite follow you.
- DISAGREEMENT: I disagree.
- EXPRESSING OPINIONS: In my opinion…
- REPHRASING: Basically, what I'm trying to say is…
- EXPRESSING OPINIONS: I think…

PARTNER B

CONVERSATION GAME

Divide into groups of 3-6. Discuss the preceding topic. Choose one person as your leader. Use as many cards as you can. Use at least three "asking for repetition" cards even if you understand everything that has been said. Record your score on a scorecard. (Appendix E)

Softening the Blow with Two Repetition Phrases

At times in conversation, it is necessary to say something that is face-threatening. Something that is face-threatening is something that may cause the person you are speaking with some discomfort. For example, the expression "Could you speak a little more loudly" implies that the person has not been speaking loudly enough, so the speaker may feel embarrassed. We have ways of making it easier to receive such face-invasive statements. Typically, we add some sort of phrase before the face-invasive phrase in order to allow the listener to prepare for the bad news. In this chapter, we can use "I don't quite follow you", a phrase that is not as face-invasive, before a more face-invasive phrase. In addition, it is almost always acceptable to place "I'm sorry" before a face-invasive statement.

TOPIC #9: OBESITY IN THE WORKPLACE

Read the passage below and answer the questions.

VOCABULARY

convict – to officially judge guilty of a crime
felon – a criminal who has committed a serious crime like murder, rape, bank robbery, assault
morbid obesity – obesity so great that it prevents normal activities
absenteeism – being absent, not coming to work or class
incentive – a motivation to do something
moral and ethical questions – questions dealing with problems such as intruding on people's privacy, respecting others as humans
divulge – to tell information that should perhaps be kept secret
hypocritical – saying one thing while doing the opposite
inherently – innate or native

Obesity has been a growing problem in many countries, and this problem is beginning to affect the way we work. In the workplace, obesity has led to an increase in people calling in sick to work and thus lower work productivity as well as a larger amount of money spent on health care. Businesses are concerned about making money, and science is now showing that obese individuals tend to produce less than workers who are in shape. Thus, there has begun to be a bit of discrimination against obese individuals. For example, one study by some researchers at Yale showed that people would rather hire a convicted felon (a person who was guilty of a serious crime) than an obese person. It is very difficult for people with morbid obesity to find jobs. Morbid obesity can be defined as someone who is so overweight that they have difficulty doing regular activities.

To combat this growing problem of obesity and therefore lower productivity for workers, some businesses have begun to implement incentive programs to encourage and motivate workers to lose weight. In an incentive program, workers may compete with other workers to lose weight, or they may attempt to lose weight, and when they do, they get some kind of bonus. However, some legal experts argue that such incentive programs raise important moral and ethical questions. Some argue that such programs invade the privacy of workers, having them divulge information they don't want to, such as their weight. But companies have argued that such "experts" are hypocritical. In US culture, it has become acceptable to encourage smokers to quit, but it is unacceptable to attack obesity.

In many industries, those that require workers to have a particular physical ability, people may be fired if they let their weight get out of control. This includes the US military. In other work places, it is not easy to require people to be of a particular weight, even when the job involves intense physical ability. One such example is a police officer. While some police chiefs (bosses) are not able to hire and fire based on weight, there have been creative methods to getting people to get into shape. In the early 2000s, a police chief in Florida, tired of working with obese officers, sent an email out encouraging his workforce to get into shape. Unfortunately, this email offended several of the officers. They thought the chief was being prejudiced and that their weight was a sensitive area that shouldn't be discussed. The memo he sent out asked the officers to get into shape, but the officers sent an anonymous letter of complaint to the chief's boss, and the chief was fired. Apparently, the chief's boss felt the chief had been too insensitive to his officers.

1 What do you think of this topic?

2 Is absenteeism a big problem, in your opinion? Are skinny workers really better than obese ones?

3 What are the best ways for a company to deal with unhealthy employees? Are incentive programs a good idea?

4 Is it fair to base whether or not to hire someone on weight?

5 Would you rather hire an obese person or a criminal?

6 Should smoking be treated as similar or different from obesity?

7 Should employers be able to tell employees anything about their weight?

8 Was it correct for the police chief to be fired for sending a memo about his officers' weight problem?

PAIR WORK

Find a partner. Answer the questions to one of the former topics you've seen. When doing so, ask your partner to rephrase what s/he has said in a face-saving way by using two "asking for repetition" cards at once.

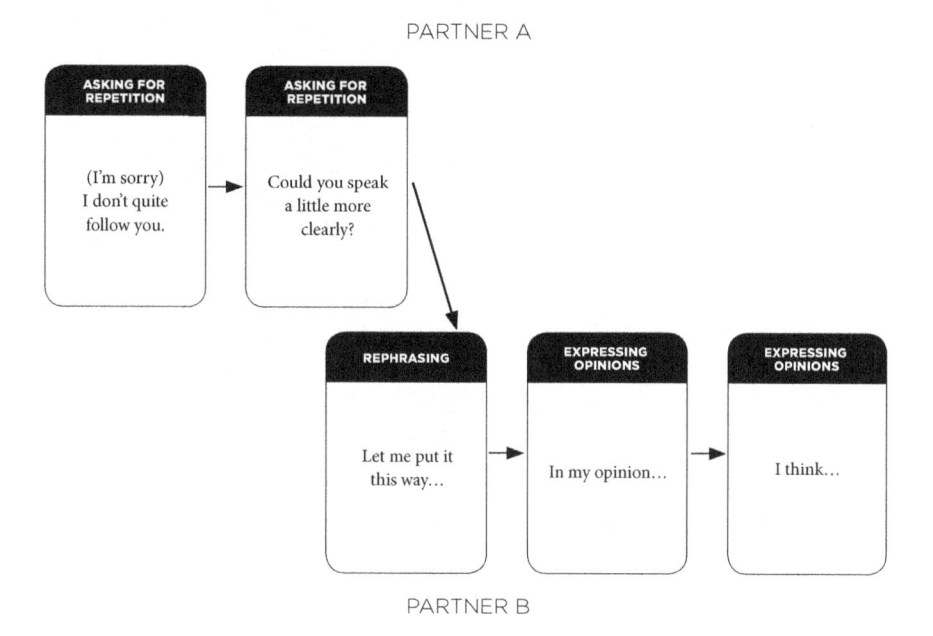

PARTNER A

ASKING FOR REPETITION	ASKING FOR REPETITION
(I'm sorry) I don't quite follow you.	Could you speak a little more clearly?

REPHRASING	EXPRESSING OPINIONS	EXPRESSING OPINIONS
Let me put it this way…	In my opinion…	I think…

PARTNER B

CONVERSATION GAME

Divide into groups of 3–6. Discuss the preceding topic. Choose one person as your leader. Attempt to discuss and answer all questions. Use as many cards as you can. Use at least five "asking for repetition" cards even if you understand everything that has been said. Try to 'soften the blow' by using two "asking for repetition" cards at once. At the end of the conversation, record your score on a scorecard. (Appendix E)

Buying Time with Two Rephrasing Phrases + Opinion

In Chapter 2 we learned how to give ourselves extra time to formulate our opinion and think about how we are going to say it by employing two opinion phrases together. This strategy was called the "In + I" strategy. Another way to buy extra time to think about what to say is by using two rephrasing cards together, but they must follow this order: 1st, "Let me put it this way…" and 2nd "Basically, what I'm trying to say is…".

TOPIC #10: FAT TAX

Read the passage below and answer the questions. Answer the questions two or three times using different words. This should increase your ability to rephrase what you have said. You will be required to rephrase things various times in this round of the conversation game.

VOCABULARY

attribute to - to see as resulting from or coming from a specific cause.
incentive - a motivation, a reason to change
consumption - eating,
tax revenue - money the government gets from taxes
generate - to create, to make
budget deficit - the amount of money the government owes
penalize - punish, give a penalty
addictive - when you cannot stop something, such as smoking or drug use

People are becoming fatter and fatter. Statistics for the US shows that last year 300,000 deaths could be attributed to obesity. In addition, health care due to obesity alone is costing the US $117 billion per year. Obesity costs the airlines money as well because it takes more fuel to move people who are obese than it does people who are not obese.

Some have begun discussing the idea of implementing a tax on junk food. They have called this tax the fat tax. Unhealthy foods are typically cheaper than healthy foods. For example, it is cheaper to have a bowl of sugary cereal or a donut than to have a salad. Thus, people may be drawn to unhealthy foods because they are cheaper than other foods.

Others claim that fattening foods are addictive. In fact, they argue, junk food contains an addictive substance. Once a person begins to eat junk food, s/he may become addicted to it, thus, continuing to eat it and becoming more and more obese.

A fat tax would do several things. First, it would provide an incentive for people to buy and to eat healthier foods. By taxing fatty foods, it is hoped that the consumption of fatty foods would decrease and the consumption of healthy foods would increase. Second, the tax revenues generated would help to reduce our budget deficit. Finally, with more people buying healthy foods, we would support our farming industry, especially those who produce vegetables and fruit.

1 Should we make a law to have a fat tax? Why or why not?

2 Would a fat tax really cause people to buy and eat healthier foods?

3 The poor in the US are the ones who largely buy fatty foods. Would a fat tax unfairly penalize the poor?

4 Is eating junk food an addiction, like alcoholism?

5 What's the best way to encourage people to eat healthy food?

PAIR WORK

Find a partner and practice asking each other to rephrase what has been said. Be sure to use two "rephrasing" cards together as shown in the diagram below. You may talk about any topic seen thus far.

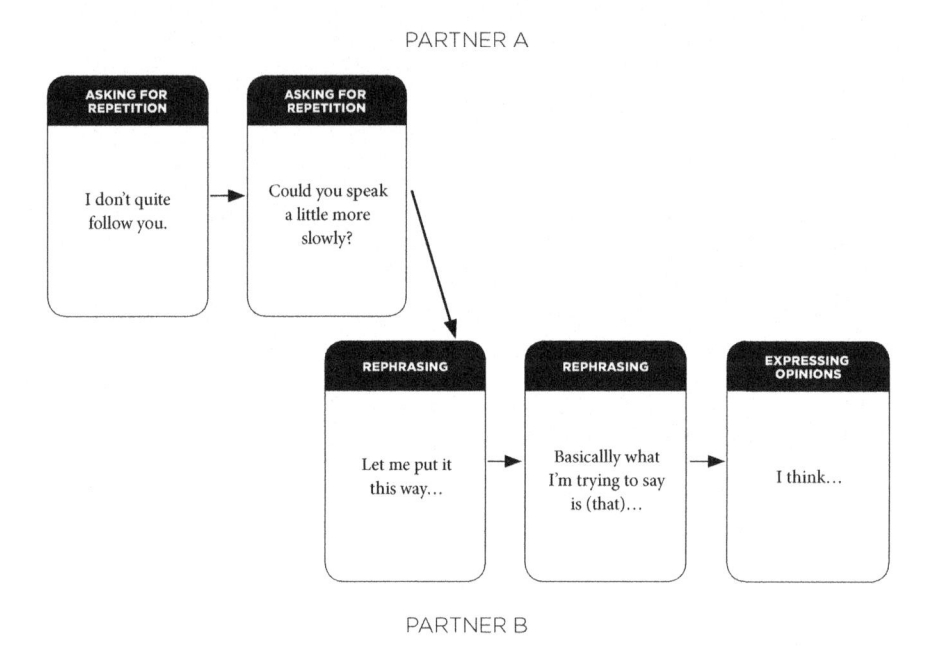

PARTNER A

ASKING FOR REPETITION	ASKING FOR REPETITION
I don't quite follow you.	Could you speak a little more slowly?

REPHRASING	REPHRASING	EXPRESSING OPINIONS
Let me put it this way…	Basicallly what I'm trying to say is (that)…	I think…

PARTNER B

CONVERSATION GAME

Divide into groups of 3–6. Discuss the preceding topic. Choose one person as your leader. Attempt to discuss and answer all questions. Use as many cards as you can. Use at least three "asking for repetition" cards even if you understand everything that has been said. At the end of the conversation, record your score on a scorecard. (Appendix E)

ELICITING PARTICIPATION AND AVOIDING A QUESTION

OBJECTIVES OF THIS CHAPTER
- Elicit responses from participants
- Avoid answering questions
- Practice all strategies seen up to this point

The leader role was introduced in Chapter 3. Leader strategies learned include introducing, concluding, and summarizing discussions. In this chapter, you will learn how to elicit responses from participants as leader, and you will learn to avoid answering questions as a participant. Eliciting responses is useful in a group of non-talkative participants. Avoiding questions is particularly useful in conversations and other situations in which you do not want to answer a question or you simply need more time to formulate an answer.

ELICITING RESPONSES AND AVOIDING QUESTIONS

As the leader of a conversation, you may often encounter times when no one is speaking or appears to want to speak. In addition, you may have unusually quiet individuals in your group. In these situations, it is often necessary to get players to give their opinions. This can be efficiently done through the use of a few memorized phrases directed either at a specific individual such as *What do you think (name)? Now, let's hear from (name)* or the group as a whole *Would anyone like to say something about that? Would anyone like to add anything? Does anyone (else) have a comment (on that)?*

In very formal speaking situations such as formal moderated discussions in graduate school or at academic conferences, it is up to the leader to elicit participation. In more casual, everyday conversations, anyone can elicit participation. For the purposes of this program, all participants can elicit participation, but it is particularly essential for the leader to elicit participation if no one is expressing opinions.

As a participant in a conversation, you may not want to give your opinion for various reasons. For example, you may not want to say what you truly think because you do not want to cause too much controversy, you may not want to disagree openly with another participant, or simply because you may not want to feel like participating. In these situations, it is often common for non-native speakers to say nothing. However, there are culturally appropriate ways of saying that you are not going to say anything, and these are expressed through memorized phrases such as *that's a good question, that's an interesting point, that's a tough question* or even a simple *good question!* Also, you may deflect the attention put on you by complimenting the questioner with phrases like *that's an interesting question* and *I'm glad you brought that up.*

Expressions

Eliciting participation
Does anyone else have a comment?
Now, let's hear from (name).
What do you think, (name)?
Would anyone like to say something about that?
Would anyone like to add something?

Avoiding a question
Good question.
That's a good question.
That's a good question, I'm glad you brought it up.
That's a difficult question.
That's an interesting question.
You've brought up a very interesting point/idea.

Basic Eliciting Participation and Avoiding Questions

Eliciting participation and avoiding questions involves two moves, one by the leader and the other by participants. The leader may ask a question, and then one or more participants may avoid this using an *avoiding the question* card. This may create a cycle as the leader uses an "eliciting participation" card followed by participants using "avoiding questions" cards. Eventually, participants will need to answer questions, even if it is not until they have run out of "avoiding question" cards, but by avoiding the question, participants gain extra time to formulate their opinions.

Turn-Taking with Eliciting Participation and Avoiding Questions

Turn-taking with eliciting participation and avoiding the question works similarly to turn-taking with opinions, agreement and disagreement in Chapter 2 and asking for repetition and rephrasing in Chapter 4. The only difference is that we use different phrases and that this turn-taking may be purely formulaic.

TOPIC #11: INVASIVE SPECIES AND EXOTIC PETS

Read the passage below and answer the questions. Although you will be attempting to avoid answering these questions, in the game, you will eventually have to answer some of them.

VOCABULARY

to opt for - to choose an option
tarantula - a large hairy spider
python - a large snake
release into the wild - let the pet go
exotic - unusual, not native
ecological - related to the environment
native - being in the environment one was born in to
thrive - to do very well
eradicate - to get rid of completely
to keep in check - to control or restrain
environmentalists - people who advocate for the environment
to smuggle - to bring something into a place illegally and secretly
to take hold - to start growing (in a certain area)
overpopulation - too many animals in one area
to prohibit - to ban

Many people these days want pets that are not your typical dog or cat, or hamster, or rabbit, or mouse. Instead, there is a growing number of people who are opting for non-traditional, or unusual, pets such as snakes, lizards, and tarantulas. Frequently, however, new owners of these pets are not prepared to take care of these pets, particularly as they grow and become adults. Thus, many of these pet owners, once they find that their baby python has become a large 18 foot snake, decide to release their pets into the wild instead of taking care of this large strange animal. In addition, some pet owners may be responsible, but their pet gets free. But regardless of how these pets get free, once they enter the environment, they may cause ecological disasters if they are not native to the area that they are kept in.

For example, in the Florida Everglades, a large swamp area, a biological war is going on between the native alligator and the non-native python. Before the arrival of the python, the alligator was the top predator. Now, however, the alligator has to compete with the python, which was introduced to the US as a pet. People buy young, small pythons, take them home, and feed them mice. These small pythons then become huge, and many pet owners let their snakes go free when they become too large to take care of conveniently. In most places in the US, these snakes quickly die because the environment is not suited for them. In Florida, however, the snakes are thriving. In response to this growing problem, wildlife officials are attempting to capture the snakes in order to protect the native species. However, it is still not known exactly how many snakes there are. Alarmingly, the snakes are mating, and each season, a female can produce up to 100 eggs, so while wildlife officials continue to try to catch and eradicate this foreign invader, the snakes are multiplying rapidly.

Two important questions related to this topic are who is to blame for the pythons and what should be done about this problem. Some believe that exotic pets should be made illegal, partially because not every pet owner can be trusted to behave in a responsible fashion. Owners of pet shops argue that they are not to blame, however, and that the owners of the pets should take responsibility. Furthermore, owners of pet shops have said that making exotic pets illegal will not stop people from getting exotic pets but rather force them to get pets that have been smuggled or brought illegally into the country. For the Everglades, however, it may be too late to solve the python problem as these snakes are multiplying at such a rapid rate already.

A similar problem is occurring in the jungles of Colombia, where a wealthy drug lord imported hippos from Africa as pets. Once this infamous drug lord was captured, his herd of hippos remained on his land. The herd had been growing at about six births per year, but as the herd approached 100, a few of the hippos started to branch out and leave the herd, starting their own herds elsewhere.

The Colombian government, in an attempt to stop an ecological disaster, began hunting the hippos, but environmentalists have decried these hunts as cruel treatment of animals. Others argue that these hippos could be very valuable if the population of hippos in Africa begins to decrease. However, others warn of an impending ecological problem in Colombia if the herd is not quickly eradicated. Some of these hippos escaped, and they began mating. Because they are not native to the area, they have no natural predators, so there is no other species to keep the hippos in check. Colombia is the perfect paradise for hippos: warm air, plenty of food, and no predators. Capturing them costs too much moneyW.

1 What is your opinion on this topic?

2 Who should be responsible for this problem? Pet owners? The owners of pet stores? The government?

3 Should the sale of exotic pets be banned? Will the ban of exotic pets really help the problem?

4 Should we protect native species? If so, what should we do?

5 In a situation like Colombia's, in which an invasive species is just starting to take hold in the environment, should the new species be eradicated completely? In other words, should all the new species be killed, or should they be allowed to live?

PAIR WORK

Find a partner you can work with. Partner A can serve as leader, and Partner B participant. Work through each question, and as each question comes up, use an "avoiding the question" card. Partner A can then use an "eliciting participation" card to get partner B to speak. After you have finished, switch roles.

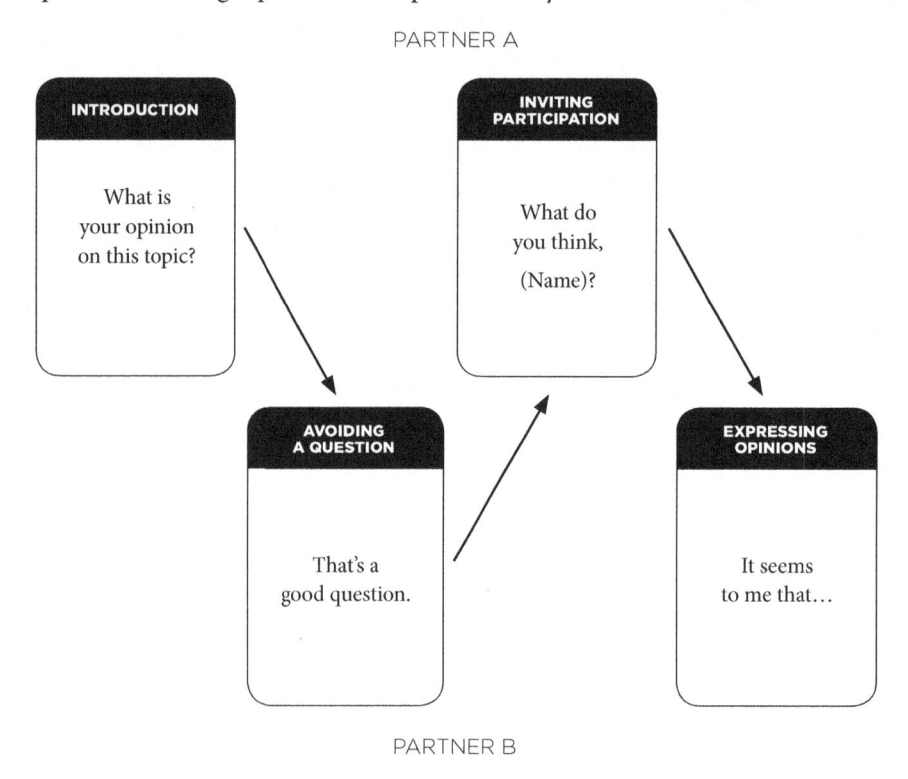

PARTNER A

INTRODUCTION
What is your opinion on this topic?

INVITING PARTICIPATION
What do you think, (Name)?

AVOIDING A QUESTION
That's a good question.

EXPRESSING OPINIONS
It seems to me that…

PARTNER B

CONVERSATION GAME

Divide into groups of 3-6. Discuss the preceding topic. Choose one person as your leader. Attempt to discuss and answer all questions. Use as many cards as you can. Leaders should use at least eight "eliciting participation" cards while participants should use at least three "avoiding a question" cards each. At the end of the conversation, record your score on a scorecard (Appendix E).

Buying Time with Avoiding the Question + Opinion

One way to buy extra time is to use as many expressions as possible before you actually have to produce creative language. Avoiding the question cards are the perfect cards for buying time as these cards give us more time to think about what we are going to say. We can use an opinion card immediately after the buying for time card.

TOPIC #12: GLOBAL WARMING

Read the passage below and answer the questions.

VOCABULARY

iceberg - large chunk of ice in the ocean
polar caps - the frozen areas of the North and South Poles
greenhouse gas - air pollution that damages the ozone
to be flawed - to have a large problem
ice age - period of time during which most of the Earth is covered in ice
to cite the fact - to reference or say a fact
drought - long period of no rain during which time crops typically die
submerge - to be under water
flood - a natural disaster involving too much water in one area
pollution - introduction of harmful and dirty substances into the environment

For the past 25 years, there has been more and more evidence that the world is warming. Major icebergs and large portions of the polar caps are beginning to melt. The sea level could eventually rise several meters, leaving many island nations completely under water and flooding other parts of the world as well. Also, weather changes could continue occurring. The sea levels have already risen several centimeters, and island nations are at risk of being completely submerged. In addition, in the last few years we have witnessed an unusually high level of natural disasters, including an increased number of hurricanes and droughts.

In 1997, the EU, the US, and Japan met and signed the Kyoto agreement, under which these political entities decided to voluntarily reduce the amount of greenhouse gases that they emit. However, the plan may be flawed because emerging nations that have not signed the treaty, such as India and China, are producing more and more of these harmful pollutants. In China, for example, many people heat their homes with coal, producing large amounts of pollution. Nations that have not typically produced much pollution are now producing an increasing amount of pollution as their economies develop. Furthermore, developed countries have not always kept their part of the agreement. For example, after having signed the agreement, the US government decided not to honor the agreement.

On the other hand, some people argue that global warming is not such a great problem. The long term weather and climate of the Earth cannot be accurately calculated, and natural events such as the collision of meteors with the Earth and the eruption of volcanoes may have far greater effects than those produced by humans. For example, in 1816, a series of large volcanic eruptions caused what has been termed as "the year of no summer." Due to several volcanic eruptions, a cloud of smoke blocked the sun, and there was no summer. During this year, many parts of the northern hemisphere suffered from food shortages as crops could not grow.

Furthermore, doubters of the global warming theory say that the Earth naturally cools and gets warmer, and that humans can do little to change this. To support this argument, they cite the fact that the temperature of the earth actually decreased between 1930 and 1970, and green house gases were being produced during those times. These doubters of global warming argue that there is no reason to do anything about this problem. They also say that in a few thousand years, the Earth will face the opposite problem: The Earth will begin cooling as it enters the next ice age.

1 What is your opinion on global warming?

2 Is it effective for some countries to reduce greenhouse gases but not all?

3 Who should be primarily held responsible for reducing greenhouse gases, only developed nations or all nations?

4 What do you think the world will look like in 50 years? Do you think island nations will disappear?

5 What will the effects of global warming, if any, be on the global population and on the global economy?

6 Can humans really do anything to influence or change the natural cycles of the climate?

PAIR WORK

Find a partner you can work with. Partner A can serve as leader, and Partner B participant. Work through each question, and as each question comes up, use an "avoiding the question" card. Partner A can then use an "eliciting participation" card to get partner B to speak. After you have finished, switch roles.

PARTNER A

INIVITING PARTICIPATION
What do you think, (Name)?

AVOIDING A QUESTION
That's an interesting question.

EXPRESSING OPINIONS
I think that…

PARTNER B

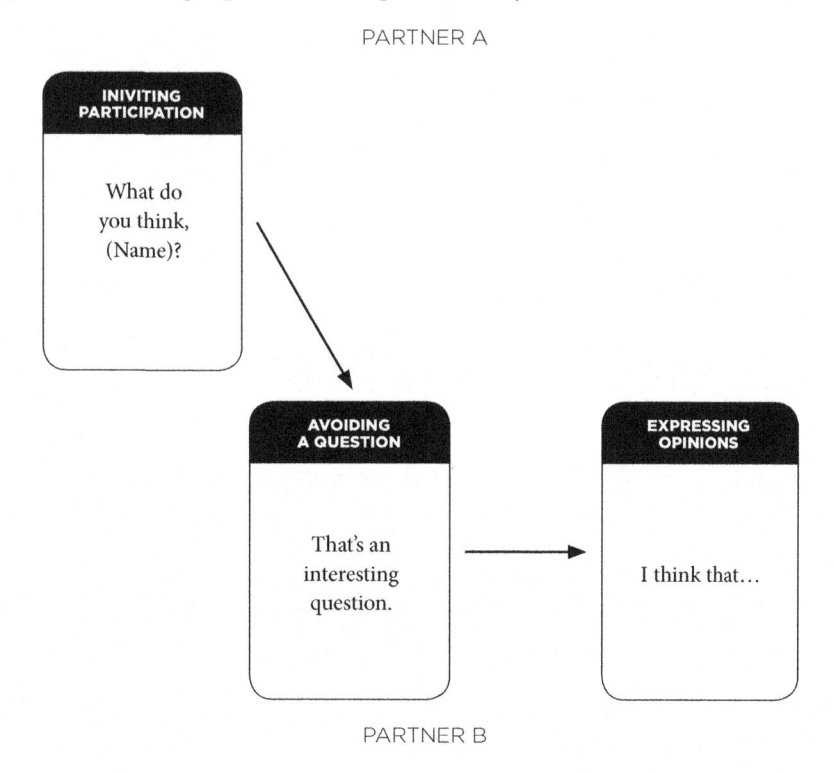

THE CONVERSATION GAME   **55**

CONVERSATION GAME

Divide into groups of 3-6. Discuss the preceding topic. Choose one person as your leader. Attempt to discuss and answer all questions. Use as many cards as you can. Leaders should use at least eight "eliciting participation" cards each. At the end of the conversation record your score on a scorecard. (Appendix E)

Buying Time with "Avoiding the Question" + "In + I"

As stated in the previous pair work section of this chapter, the more expressions you can use, the more time you can buy for yourself. You can combine an avoiding the question card with the "In + I" strategy (seen in Chapter 2) to give yourself even more time before you have to formulate your opinion.

TOPIC #13: THE ECOLOGICAL IMPACT OF GREEN ENERGY

Read the passage below and answer the questions.

VOCABULARY

fossil fuels – sources of energy from the earth that are not renewable such as oil, coal, and gas
renewable – able to be replenished or will not run out
harness – to tame, to take from nature and make usable to humankind
alternative energy – sources of energy other than fossil fuels
wind turbine – windmill or machine that produces electricity from the wind
oppose – to be against
eye sore – ugly to see
migratory path – pattern of migration – travel of animals
hydroelectric – creating energy through water dams
extinctions – all of a particular species dies off
impact – influence
green energy – renewable energy can be replenished
to be justified – to have a good reason for
ecological – related to the environment

Green energy, or renewable energy, refers to sources of energy like the sun, wind, and water that do not pollute and will not run out. Fossil fuels, on the other hand, are energy sources like gas, coal, and oil that pollute and will eventually be completely used up. As the world continues to develop, the prices of fossil fuels such as gas and coal continue to rise. As they do, countries are beginning to consider alternative sources of energy. The main sources of such alternative energy is green energy.

Green energy is energy that does not pollute the environment. Examples of green energy include solar power, energy gotten from the sun, wind power, energy harnessed from the wind via windmills, geothermal power, power gotten from the heat of the earth, and hydroelectric power, or powers gotten damming large rivers. Governments and corporations are creating large projects and structures that can harness these natural sources of power. For example, the US is planning on building a massive wind turbine, or windmill, project off the coast of Texas. This project will generate electricity for over 200, 000 homes, yet the project has gathered a lot of opposition from two different groups.

The first group that opposes this project is comprised of people who live in the area. They complain that the wind turbines will be one gigantic eye sore, dirtying the beautiful scenery. They don't want to have to look at the windmill project. A second group, a bird conservation group, is also unhappy with the project. They say that the turbines are going to be built in the migratory path of many birds that travel to Mexico in the Fall and back to the US in the Spring. They argue that thousands of birds will be killed since the turbines are directly in the birds' path. In fact, they argue that there could be no worse place for the project, but there has been little scientific evidence to back up their claims.

Similar concerns are often raised over hydroelectric projects. To generate hydroelectric power, governments have to build huge dams on rivers. The creation of these dams often disrupts the migratory patterns of fish, perhaps leading them to extinction. Also, the dams may flood usable land upstream, so people often lose their houses and farmland when a government chooses to construct a dam. Nevertheless, many argue that the creation of energy may always impact the environment in some ways and that these greener types of energy are preferable to traditional types of energy such as coal and oil.

1 What is your opinion on this topic?

....
....
....
....

2 Which, in your opinion, is worse: the green energy projects listed above or the continued use of gas and coal? Why?

....
....
....
....

3 Builders of wind turbines accuse environmentalists of never being satisfied: Environmentalists want neither fossil fuels nor alternative sources? Is this accusation justified?

4 Is it inevitable (unavoidable) that we destroy nature's beauty, or nature in general, to create energy?

5 Are green energy projects such as wind turbine farms and dams beautiful in their own ways?

6 Think about the future of humankind. How will we be getting energy 50 years from now? 100 years from now? 200 years from now?

PAIR WORK

Find a partner. Partner A can serve as leader, and partner B participant. Work through each question, and as each question comes up, use an "avoiding the question" + the "In + I" strategy. Thus, partner B should be using three cards each time s/he answers a question. Partner A can then use an "eliciting participation" card to get partner B to speak. After you have finished, switch roles.

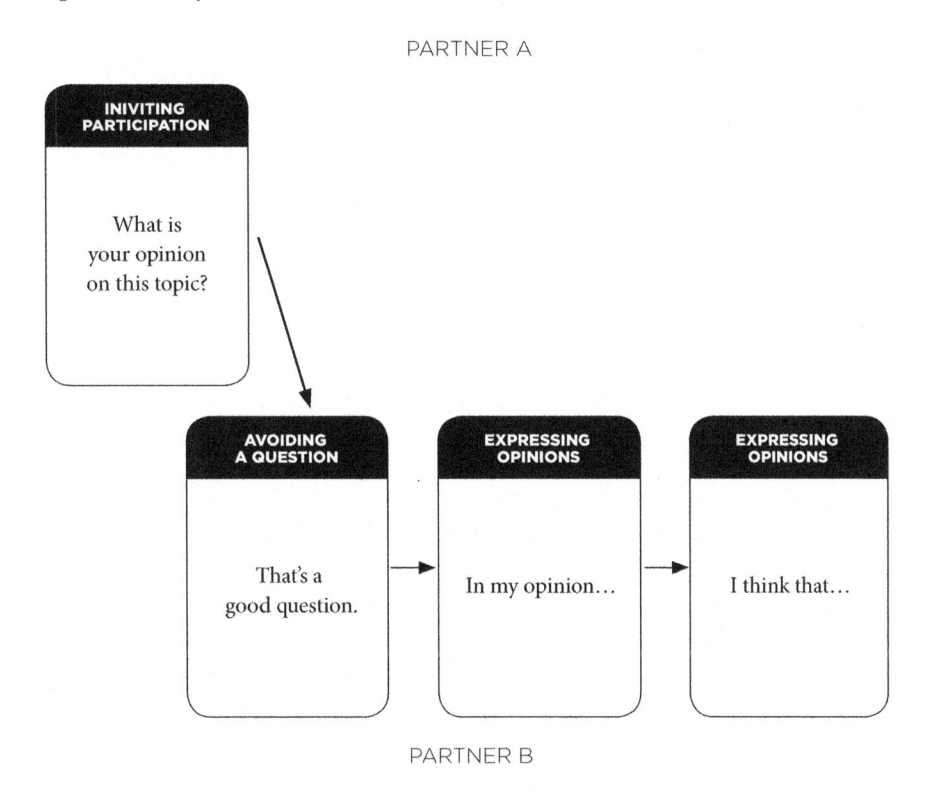

PARTNER A

INVITING PARTICIPATION
What is your opinion on this topic?

AVOIDING A QUESTION
That's a good question.

EXPRESSING OPINIONS
In my opinion…

EXPRESSING OPINIONS
I think that…

PARTNER B

CONVERSATION GAME

Divide into groups of 3-6. Discuss the preceding topic. Choose one person as your leader. Attempt to discuss and answer all questions. Use as many cards as you can. Leaders should use at least eight "eliciting participation" cards while participants should use at least three "avoiding a question" cards each. At the end of the conversation, record your score on a scorecard. (Appendix E)

INTERRUPTIONS AND MANAGING THE CONVERSATION

OBJECTIVES OF THIS CHAPTER
- Keep participants on topic
- Interrupt other participants politely
- Begin a new idea in a discussion politely
- Use several cards in a row to smoothly and seamlessly move the discussion through the different discussion questions

One important skill for conversations in English is the ability to interrupt another. At times, we may converse with individuals who dominate discussions and thus we must interrupt in order to say anything. Also, it is common for some people to interrupt frequently in conversation. Some English speakers actually expect the people they speak with to interrupt them when they speak. The acceptability of interrupting varies greatly among people, and you will have to make your own judgment on how much to use interruption. For the purpose of this game, however, you will be expected to interrupt your co-players. The game aims to teach you this necessary skill.

As players, you will be interrupting each other in order to gain the floor. Later in chapter 7, you will be taught to speak at length. During this time, it will be necessary for you to interrupt to get into the conversation. You will learn three expressions for interrupting. You will also learn two expressions that are used by leaders to manage the conversation. You will add these cards to the expression "Let's move on to the next/last question" from Chapter 3. Leaders will be taught a strategy for interrupting participants when they begin to talk about something other than the topic at hand.

Expressions

Managing the Conversation

I think we're getting off the subject

Let's try to stick to the topic of this discussion.

Interruption

Excuse me, can/may I interrupt you for a second?

May/can I interrupt you for a second?

Let me interrupt just for a second.

Interrupting

Interrupting can be very face-invasive. In other words, it is often considered rude. However, sometimes you will be in a situation in which there seems to be no way to enter the conversation because one member is dominating the conversation. Also, if you are the leader, you will need to interrupt when individuals get off the topic. In these situations, the skill of interruption is essential.

For the purposes of this program, you will practice interrupting your conversation partners even though this may not be commonly done in your culture or comfortable. The goal is to acquire this important skill so when you need it, you can use it. In this first section, you will learn to interrupt another speaker's opinion. This may be necessary if someone is talking at length about something unrelated to the topic or when time is running out and you need to say something important. Note that it is important to give a slight pause after the interruption phrase to allow the other person to acknowledge that it is okay to interrupt them.

TOPIC #14: SCHOOL CHOICE

Read the passage below and answer the questions.

VOCABULARY

free-market – *anything based on the idea of the free and unre-stricted buying and selling of products or services. The free-market system is based on the idea that competition for buyers will make sellers improve their products and services.*

In most countries, public school attendance is typically determined by where one lives. People who live in a particular neighborhood go to that neighborhood's school. In other countries, school choice may be determined by performance on tests. Regardless, which school one attends is rarely a choice, and thus schools, which are funded by the government, do not have to compete for students.

An alternative to this system was proposed in the 1950s by a famous economist named Milton Friedman. He argued that if students were allowed to choose the school they wanted to attend, schools would have to compete for students. Thus, schools in this free-market type system would naturally need to produce better results or products—better education—than they would under the traditional system. Theoretically, schools would provide better services for students as they competed for students.

There are different kinds of school choice systems that have been implemented in different places, so it is difficult to compare them. In some countries where there are poorer families, such as in the US, there are special schools that students who are poor and need to work or are perhaps parents already, can go to study and finish high school more quickly than they could in a typical school. Also, there are schools that have been termed "alternative schools," which allow students to study what they want when they want. Thus, rarely are there classes but rather study places and times, and students are responsible for finishing their studies.

There are various ways that school choice has been implemented in different places. One system is a voucher system. In this system, each student gets a piece of paper called a voucher which gives them a certain amount of money or credit that they can spend on tuition for any school. Students can use that voucher to go to almost any public school for free, or they can go to a private school and pay the difference between the voucher and the cost of the private school.

The opponents of school choice argue that these systems take funding away from the public schools. Furthermore, they argue, voucher systems favor the rich, allowing wealthier students to go to private schools while poorer students are still stuck in public schools. A second argument against school choice is that schools are not performing any better under the choice system than they were under the traditional system, although there is some evidence from Chile, at least, to counteract that claim. A final argument against school choice is that they help pay for religious schools. Many in the US claim that since school is funded by taxpayers, these schools should not be teaching religion. Regardless of one's view, however, charter schools and voucher systems have been gaining in popularity in the last 20 years. It is unlikely that they are going to go away.

1 What is your opinion on this topic?

2 In your opinion, can free market principles be successfully used to reform education? Why or why not?

3 What are some of the problems with school choice? Are these serious?

4 Should special schools be made for students with special needs, such as teenage mothers, children of single mothers, students with learning disabilities, etc?

5 What do you think would be the best way to reform public schools?

6 Do you think an alternative school system in which students studied independently would work in your country? Why or why not?

PAIR WORK

Find a partner and alternate expressing opinions and interrupting. Partner A should express an opinion on the above topic or any other topic seen thus far, and then partner B should attempt to interrupt Partner A. Switch roles after you have practiced this several times.

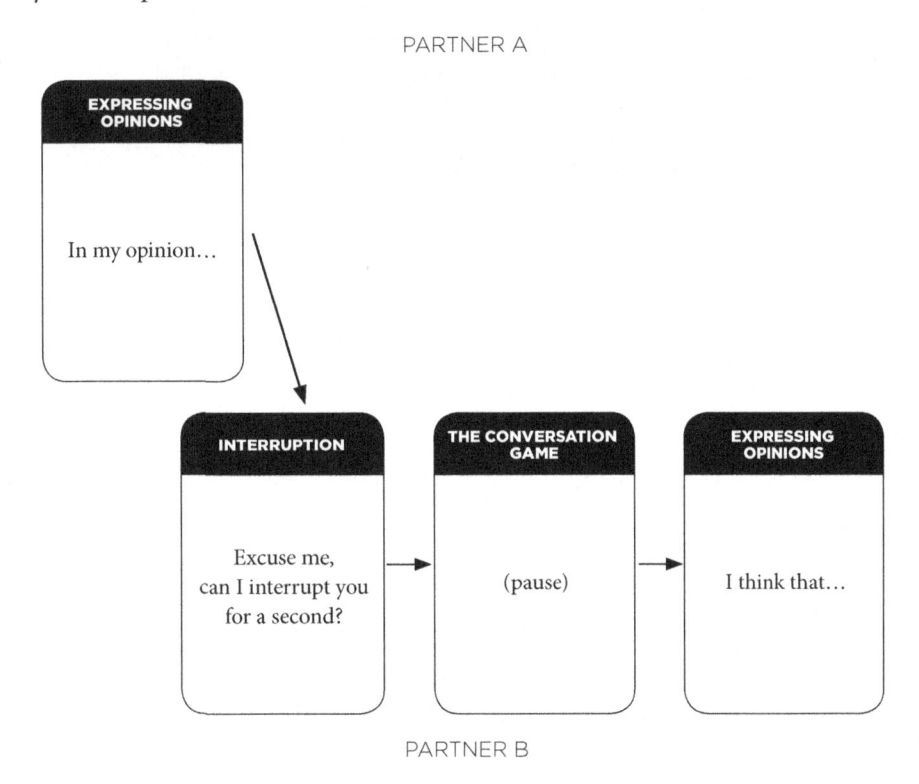

PARTNER A

EXPRESSING OPINIONS
In my opinion…

INTERRUPTION
Excuse me, can I interrupt you for a second?

THE CONVERSATION GAME
(pause)

EXPRESSING OPINIONS
I think that…

PARTNER B

CONVERSATION GAME

Divide into groups of 3-6. Discuss the preceding topic. Choose one person as your leader. Try to discuss and answer all questions, using as many "interruption" cards as possible. Once you have finished, record the number of cards you used on a scorecard. (Appendix E)

Going off on Tangents and Reining in Tangents

A tangent is a part of the conversation that is only very slightly related to the topic. As a leader of a conversation, it is important to bring the conversation back to the main topic. One way to do this is to interrupt and then explicitly state that the conversation has gone off on a tangent.

TOPIC #15: HOME SCHOOLING

Read the passage below and answer the questions.

VOCABULARY

academic achievement - how much someone learns, how well they perform on tests or what their grades are
extracurricular activities - activities that occur outside normal school hours such as sports and hobbies
to opt - to select one from among two or more choices
to be inconclusive - not to be definite, or settled
peer - someone of the same age and/or status; someone who is equal in status

Homeschooling occurs when parents keep their children at home and teach them school subjects at home instead of sending them to a public or private school. Homeschooling has become popular in developed countries, and particularly in the US. In 1984, only 27% of the population approved of homeschooling, but that number has increased to about 50% today. There are many reasons parents choose to home school their children. An often cited reason is distance: many families live in remote areas that are located far from the nearest school, so homeschooling is one of the few options available to these families. More commonly, however, parents choose to keep their children at home due to either religious or academic reasons. For example, some religions don't believe in evolution, so parents do not want their children learning about evolution in school. Other parents feel that public schools do not provide a very high quality of education, and they feel that they can provide their children with a better education at home.

Proponents of homeschooling cite various reasons for why homeschooling is better than traditional schooling. First, they claim that children learn more at home. As the argument goes, schools only provide a one-size-fits-all service for children. In other words, teachers give classes in only one way, and instruction is rarely catered to the learning styles, personalities, etc. of individual students. Homeschooling allows students to work individually on whatever they are interested in. A second argument of homeschoolers is that public schools these days are dangerous. In 1997, 12 students were killed at Columbine high school when two shooters went from classroom to classroom killing students.

Opponents also have their arguments. First, they question statistics of whether homeschoolers perform better academically than those in traditional schools. Many states do not require homeschoolers to be tested, and in those states in which students are tested, results are often inconclusive. Second, opponents state that homeschoolers are not socialized into the community or the nation. In school, students are exposed to students from various backgrounds, including those of different religions, socio-economic backgrounds, and ethnic and racial backgrounds. While parents of homeschoolers often attempt to have their children meet with the peers outside of the home, these peers are frequently other homeschoolers and are likely to have similar backgrounds. Finally, opponents question whether parents are qualified to teach their children. Teachers go through rigorous training before entering the classroom, and are typically only certified to teach a given subject or grade levels, but parents who keep their kids at home have to teach their children everything, from how to spell all the way up to calculus.

To conclude, homeschooling is a growing trend in the US and other developed nations, but this trend raises serious questions. It is unquestionable that the current public school systems need changing: students' performance is deteriorating. However, the question as to whether or not homeschooling is a good option remains unanswered.

1 What is your opinion on this topic?

2 What are the advantages of homeschooling? Do you agree that these are advantages?

3 What are the advantages and/or disadvantages to traditional schooling, both public and private?

4 Do you feel it is important for children to have contact with peers of different backgrounds? Why or why not? Does homeschooling prevent or inhibit this?

5 Would you home school your own children? Why or why not?

6 What do you think the future of homeschooling will be? Will this trend increase? Do you think there will be greater regulation of this?

TANGENTIAL QUESTION

1 What do you think about religious schools?

PAIR WORK

With a partner, practice the conversation strategy above. Partner A should express an opinion on a tangential question, and partner B should come in and rein in the tangent.

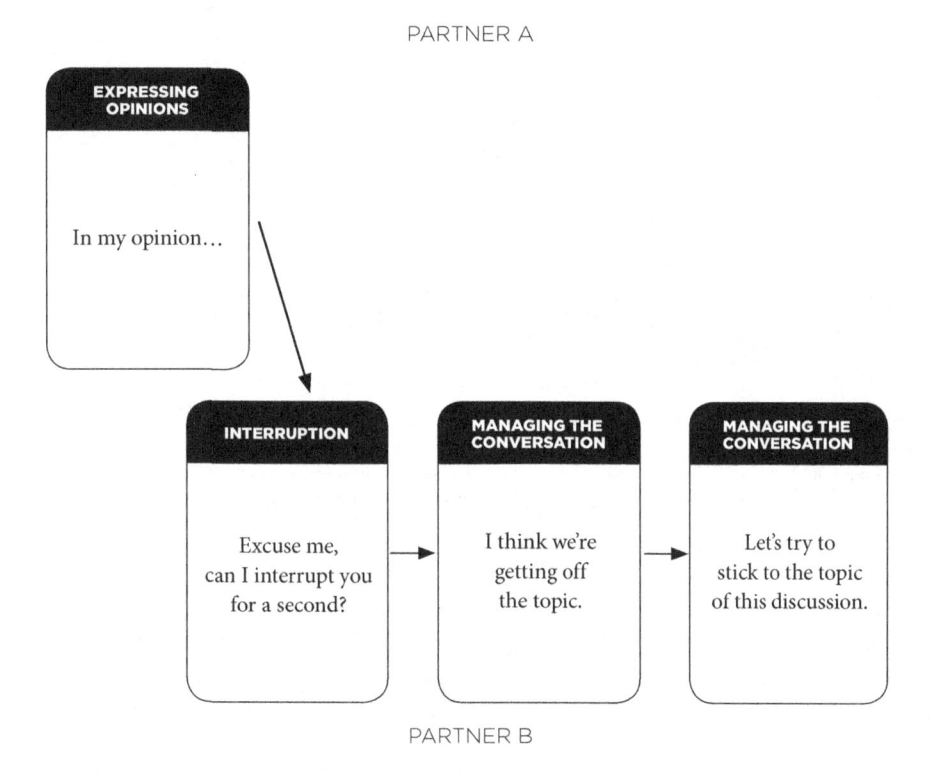

PARTNER A

EXPRESSING OPINIONS

In my opinion...

INTERRUPTION

Excuse me, can I interrupt you for a second?

MANAGING THE CONVERSATION

I think we're getting off the topic.

MANAGING THE CONVERSATION

Let's try to stick to the topic of this discussion.

PARTNER B

CONVERSATION GAME

Divide into groups of 3-6. Discuss the preceding topic. Choose one person as your leader. Attempt to discuss and answer all questions. Use as many cards as you can. Once you have finished your discussion, record the number of cards you used on the scorecard. (Appendix E)

Interrupting + Reining in Tangents + Moving the Discussion Along

In previous chapters, we have seen that it is possible to combine several phrases to speak more at length. We have typically done this to buy time or to open up the floor. Here, we will use several cards at once. This is a more sophisticated move. We will interrupt, rein in tangents, and then move to the next question all at once.

TOPIC #16: SCHOOL UNIFORMS

Read the passage below and answer the questions.

In many countries it is common for schools to require children to wear uniforms. In fact, this practice is common in many parts of the world, from South Korea to Great Britain, from Costa Rica to Australia. In other countries, however, such as the United States and France, this practice is not so common and even controversial.

There are various advantages to requiring students to wear uniforms to school. First, this practice creates a sense of community and school pride. Students who wear uniforms have a greater sense of belonging. However, some argue that requiring students to wear uniforms suppresses students´ freedom of choice and individuality. Also, when students wear uniforms, teachers may fail to recognize individual talents, abilities, or characteristics of different students.

One practical benefit to the wearing of uniforms is that students are easily identifiable as belonging to their school when outside the school. Thus, they may be encouraged to act more responsibly and courteously. However, when children of rival schools encounter each other, they also easily recognize each other and thus uniforms may encourage fights and bullying.

When students leave school and enter the work force, they will likely be required to wear particular clothes. This may be a uniform, but it may also be corporate dress. By requiring students to wear uniforms, schools help train students in dressing according to set standards. Nevertheless, dress in the business world is becoming more relaxed.

One advantage to use of uniforms is that teachers can easily check to see whether students are maintaining appropriate dress. However, some argue that uniforms are often inappropriate, with clothes being too hot for summer and too cool for winter. Also, female students often complain of always having to wear skirts.

Parents may benefit from the practice of requiring students to wear uniforms because they can save money on clothes. In addition, uniforms help to hide gaps between rich and poor students. However, uniforms can be expensive, and students need clothes to wear when they are not attending class.

1 What is your general opinion on school uniforms? Is this a beneficial practice? Why or why not?

2 Do uniforms encourage students to act more responsibly when they are outside of school, or do they promote school rivalries?

3 Do school uniforms help students focus more on school and less on fashion? Why or why not?

4 In your opinion, is the practice of wearing school uniforms beneficial to parents in any way?

TANGENTIAL QUESTIONS

Now, answer these questions that are unrelated to the main topic. You will practice giving your opinion topics not related to the main topic while giving the leader the opportunity to practice managing the conversation.

1 Should teachers have to wear particular uniforms or types of clothing?

2 Should office workers or workers at companies be required to wear uniforms?

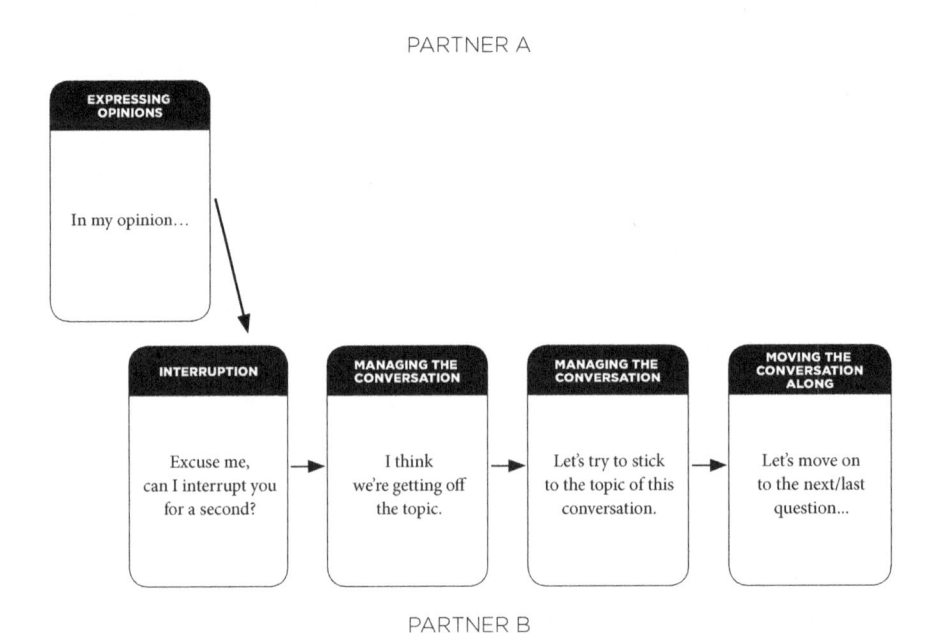

PARTNER A

EXPRESSING OPINIONS
In my opinion…

INTERRUPTION	MANAGING THE CONVERSATION	MANAGING THE CONVERSATION	MOVING THE CONVERSATION ALONG
Excuse me, can I interrupt you for a second?	I think we're getting off the topic.	Let's try to stick to the topic of this conversation.	Let's move on to the next/last question…

PARTNER B

Sample Dialogue:
A: ***In my opinion***, I think that school uniforms should be used.
B: ***Excuse me, can I interrupt you for a second***?
B: *I think we're getting off the topic.*
B: *Let's try to stick to the topic of this discussion.*
B: *Let's move on to the next question.*
B: *In your opinion, can free market principles be successfully used to reform education? Why or why not?*

PAIR WORK
With a partner, take turns expressing opinions on tangents (going off on tangents and the interruption + reining in tangents + managing the discussion strategy).

CONVERSATION GAME
Divide into groups of 3-6. Discuss the preceding topic. Choose one person as your leader. Attempt to discuss and answer all questions. Use as many cards as you can. Once you have finished the conversation, record the number of cards you used on a scorecard. (Appendix E)

EXTENDED TURNS AND COUNTERARGUMENTS

OBJECTIVES OF THIS CHAPTER:
- Introduce the strategy of opinion runs
- Practice fluency
- Speak 60 seconds without stopping
- Acknowledge counterarguments
- Minimize counterarguments

Thus far, we have been concerned with memorized phrases and short, creative sentences. We have focused on using formulaic phrases in conversations correctly and mastering these strategies, and we have been particularly interested in mastering short adjacency pairs with a rapid succession of turn-taking. We have also been using other language and more creative language to express our opinions. However, if playing the game correctly, you should not have spoken much longer than a few seconds at a time. We have left to one side the issue of longer units of speech. While these longer units of speech are not the focus of this book, this chapter is focused on assisting you at speaking for longer periods of time using some of the phrases you have already acquired.

In longer blocks of speaking, there will typically be alternating segments of formulaic language with more creative language. One way this is done is through *opinion runs*. An opinion run is a longer segment of speech during which an individual alternates between using pre-fabricated opinion expressions such as "in my opinion" or "I think" with more creative expressions. By using the memorized phrases on the cards, you will obtain some time to think about the statements you are going to make. The statements are made at the creative level of language and are often difficult to produce. Switching between the two levels of language should enable you to increase your speed of speaking while limiting the amount of time you spend thinking about each topic. You will likely need to practice opinion runs at home and with classmates to obtain the full benefit of this speaking strategy.

Expressions

Acknowledging and Minimizing Counterarguments
   (But) Even if…
   (But) Even though…

Re-Emphasizing One's Opinion
   I still…

Opinion Runs

An opinion run is basically cycling between formulaic opinion phrases and more creative statements. This is a useful strategy for expressing longer, more in-depth opinions because when saying the formulaic phrases, we have time to think of what to put in the creative utterances. There are various ways the opinion phrases seen in Chapter 2 can be combined in opinion runs, and we are also going to add some other phrases to allow for more sophisticated ways of expressing opinions, namely for minimizing counterarguments. Also, we've added "but" to the phrase "I can't help thinking that …". We have done this because the "I can't help thinking that" typically introduces some sort of negative opinion or disagreement related to the current topic and is thus introduced with "but". This is a common pattern in English discourse, both written and spoken.

TOPIC #17: FACE-RECOGNITION SOFTWARE

Read the passage below and answer the questions.

After 9/11, the US government poured money into technologies that would help them identify terrorists. Due to this threat to the country, the US government and companies began spending a great deal of money on technologies that might help prevent future incidents. One such technology that was developed in response to this threat was called PittPatt, a facial recognition program that is able to take a picture and, using directories, databases, and websites on the Internet, find the person's identity. In other words, by simply taking a picture of an individual it is possible to find out the exact identity of that individual including name, phone number, address, place of work, and even social security number. On the Internet is stored a wide range of photos of people, from Facebook profile pictures, to snap shots taken by other people, to various school and work directories. While it is possible to try to delete some or even most of these photos, it is impossible to completely remove all of one's photos from the Internet. Once the Internet knows your face, it never forgets.

The developers of this technology tested it out by taking snap shots of people on a street and also by looking at pictures of people on dating websites. They then input the photos into the software program which accessed the Internet to find the identities of the individuals. Within about one minute, the program was able to identify almost all photos. While the initial intention of the software was to find terrorists, the FBI and other governmental agencies are considering using it to find criminals. This use of this software is promising, but other uses are questionable or even downright scary.

In some countries, citizens or the police have used similar software to attempt to identify rioters and demonstrators. This use naturally invokes Orwellian scenarios: governments might use the software to identify peaceful demonstrators, or people who vote a certain way, or do certain things, or to track citizens in all their actions, the ultimate tool of a Big Brother. Thus, governments could more easily control their citizens by restricting their movements, imprisoning or punishing people who attend particular meetings or attend peaceful demonstrations. Another possibility is unquestionably sinister: the use of this technology by criminals. Criminals might be able to assume people's identities.

More recently, powerful technology companies like Facebook and Google have introduced their own versions of facial recognition software. These programs enable anyone to discover the identities of people from the Internet. The European Union is currently threatening legal action against Facebook for allowing such an invasion of privacy, and some think rightfully so, but the question remains as to whether or not such technology should exist, and if it should, who should be allowed to use it.

Answer the following questions using the format given. Make at least one creative statement after each opinion expression.

1 What do you think of this topic?

In my opinion,

I think that

My sense is that

(but) I can't help thinking that

It seems to me that

2 Are the uses of facial recognition software beneficial or dangerous?
Is it like a new nuclear weapon on a personal level?

In my opinion,

I think that

My sense is that

(but) I can't help thinking that

It seems to me that

3 Should governments act to restrict the use of such technology? In my opinion, I think that

My sense is that

(but) I can't help thinking that

It seems to me that

4 Should such technology even exist? If so, who should be allowed to use it? Only governments? Companies? Individual citizens? If individual citizens use this software ...

In my opinion,

I think that

My sense is that

(but) I can't help thinking that

It seems to me that

5 Compare the invention of the nuclear bomb and the possibilities for evil to that of facial recognition software.

In my opinion,

I think that

My sense is that

(but) I can't help thinking that

It seems to me that

6 Is the Internet a Big Brother, all-knowing (omniscient)?

In my opinion,

I think that

My sense is that

(but) I can't help thinking that

It seems to me that

7 "Once the Internet knows your face, it never forgets." How does this quote illustrate the ways life has changed since the advent of the Internet?

In my opinion,

I think that

My sense is that

(but) I can't help thinking that

It seems to me that

PAIR WORK
Work with a partner. Take turns expressing extended turns with opinion runs. Try to speak 60 seconds without stopping.

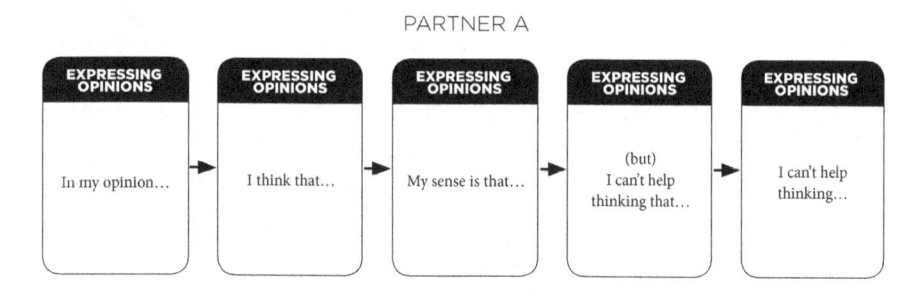

PARTNER A

EXPRESSING OPINIONS	EXPRESSING OPINIONS	EXPRESSING OPINIONS	EXPRESSING OPINIONS	EXPRESSING OPINIONS
In my opinion...	I think that...	My sense is that...	(but) I can't help thinking that...	I can't help thinking...

CONVERSATION GAME
Divide into groups of 3-6. Discuss the preceding topic. Choose one person as your leader. Attempt as many opinion runs as possible. Use as many cards as you can. At the end of the conversation, record your score on a scorecard. (Appendix E)

Acknowledging and Minimizing Counterarguments
Often when expressing long opinions, it is necessary to acknowledge a counterargument, an argument that is against what we think or believe. After bringing up a counterargument, it is important to acknowledge and minimize the counterargument. One formulaic way we do this is with the phrases "but even if..." + "I still...". In this combination of moves, we quickly address the counterargument but state that we still hold to our original opinion.

Sample Dialogue:

A: **_Even if_** global warming continues, we'll be fine.

A: **_Even if_** my boss is monitoring me (I don't know if s/he is), it shouldn't matter because I follow the rules
at work.

A: **_Even if_** people are able to make new laws to limit companies spying on employees, I don't think it will have much effect.

TOPIC #18: ONLINE MAPS

Read the passage below and answer the questions.

There are virtual replicas of the globe that exist on the Internet. Users can simply type in a particular location and see images of that location. Companies have spent a great deal of effort and money on mapping and updating this virtual globe to make sure it has the best resolution of most areas in the world, and indeed, they have been greatly successful in capturing pictures of most of the earth.

There are various positive uses of this new technology. In education, for example, teachers have been able to integrate mobile images of places in the world that they want to talk about. Thus, for example, when studying about China and the Great Wall, a teacher can show students images of the Great Wall. This program is also excellent for helping people see a place before arriving so they have an idea what it will look like. Another new feature of virtual maps is keeping track of traffic in cities in real time, so commuters can plan their travel around traffic jams. Importantly, these maps allow people to see the destruction of areas hit by natural disasters. Other less dramatic positive uses include things like being able to find directions to local stores, restaurants, schools, and libraries.

However, this new technology has several particularly negative disadvantages. It seems that criminals may always find a way to use technology to their advantage. Virtual maps are no exception. The US, Indian, and Israeli governments have been particularly critical of these maps, arguing that terrorists can use information on them to plan attacks. In the UK, for example, thieves used online maps to find churches with lead ceilings, and they then stole the lead from the ceilings and sold it. Thus, it is easy to imagine how thieves could use digital maps to access information about your personal residence.

And then there are uses of online maps that may be both beneficial and harmful. One example is the use of this technology to broadcast the daily happenings of a primitive Amazonian tribe called the Tumbira, a group of about 100 people who subsist on hunting and gathering. In its attempt to map the world, one company has sent a small team into the Amazon to show this tribe to the world. Of course, this is of great educational value to students who study anthropology, but it is also a grave invasion of privacy of these individuals who have no modern technology. How can these simple hunter-gatherers understand that images of them may be stored in cyber space for a near eternity?

1 What is your opinion on this topic? What do you think about this technology?

In my opinion,

I think (that)

(But) even if

I (still) think (that)

It seems to me (that)

2 Is it acceptable for a corporation to take both aerial and street-level pictures of private residences (think about your own home) and put that on the Internet for anyone to see?

In my opinion,

I think (that)

(But) even if

I (still) feel (that)

It seems to me (that)

3 There are several positive uses of this technology. Do these positive uses justify the implementation of this technology?

In my opinion,

I think that

(But) even if

My sense is (still) that

It seems to me that

4 Some of the disadvantages of this technology are truly scary. What should be done about these dangers to protect the public, if anything?

In my opinion,

I think (that)

(But) even if

It (still) seems to me (that)

It seems to me (that)

5 What do you think about broadcasting the private lives of the Tumbira?

In my opinion,

I think (that)

(But) even if

I (still) think (that)

It seems to me (that)

PAIR WORK

Find a partner and take turns creating opinion runs. In your opinion runs, be sure to use the acknowledging and minimizing counterarguments strategy. Try to speak for 60 seconds without stopping.

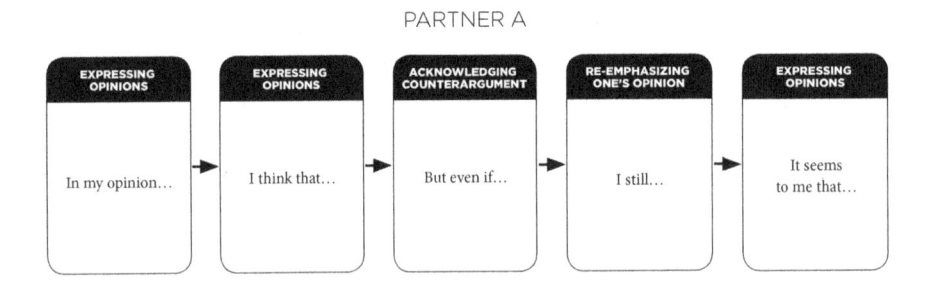

PARTNER A

EXPRESSING OPINIONS	EXPRESSING OPINIONS	ACKNOWLEDGING COUNTERARGUMENT	RE-EMPHASIZING ONE'S OPINION	EXPRESSING OPINIONS
In my opinion…	I think that…	But even if…	I still…	It seems to me that…

Sample Dialogue

A: **What do you think?**

B: **In my opinion**, I think that facial recognition software is not a huge problem. I think that the threat of criminals stealing my identity is not great. **But even if** criminals are able to steal someone's identity using this software, **I still** feel that it's not a great problem. It seems to me that the government would easily be able to catch criminals using other people's identities.

CONVERSATION GAME

Divide into groups of 3-6. Discuss the preceding topic. Choose one person as your leader. Attempt to discuss and answer all questions. Use as many cards as you can, but attempt as many opinion runs as possible, and, in particular, try to use the *acknowledging and minimizing counterarguments* strategy. At the end of the conversation, record your score on a scorecard. (Appendix E)

Acknowledging and Minimizing Counterarguments II

This strategy is almost the same as the previous one, but with the phrase "even though" instead of "even if". "Even though" expresses something that is certain—it is something that happened, while "even if" addresses a possibility.

Sample Dialogue:

A: ***Even though*** the earth has warmed, ***I still*** don't believe in global warming.

A: ***Even though*** my boss is monitoring me (I know s/he does it), I don't care.

A: ***Even though*** some places in the US have made new laws limiting companies' ability to spy on employees, these laws have had little effect.

TOPIC #19: WORKPLACE SURVEILLANCE

Read the passage below and answer the questions.

VOCABULARY

surveillance - being watched, spied upon
court order - an official order by a judge
disgruntled - unhappy with
betray - to deceive or be disloyal to

"There is no such thing as privacy anymore." Due to the increasing amount of technology that surrounds us, we have relatively little to no privacy anymore. This is particularly true in the workplace, where employers often have video cameras that record what goes on and computer programs that monitor what we do on our work computers. Some employers even have GPS devices in company-issued phones and computers that track our movements even when we are away from work.

This problem is compounded by the fact that we increasingly need to conduct personal business from work. People are working longer hours these days, and in families it is typical for both partners to work due to financial obligations. Thus, it may be necessary for parents to use work time and work phones to call teachers to discuss their children's behavior, etc. Employers, however, are not always happy about this, particularly if it disrupts work time, and, due to recent technological advances, they have been able to monitor what their employees are doing at work. Furthermore, many companies issue their employees work phones and computers, and companies use these devices to monitor their workers. An important question that this trend has brought up is how much surveillance, if any, should companies be allowed to engage in?

Another reason employers may want to monitor their employees is to protect company secrets. While many threats of leaking company secrets come from the outside—hackers and such—the more dangerous types of attacks come from the inside from workers who have become disgruntled and intend to betray their company. For example, in 2010, a private in the US military was disgruntled with US military actions in Iraq and Afghanistan, and so he stole diplomatic cables and sent them to an online organization to be published in various European newspapers. Thus, the ability of even low-level employees to access high-level information is serious, and perhaps serious enough for companies and governments to want to monitor their workers.

1 What is your opinion on this topic?

In my opinion,

I think (that)

(But) even though

I (still) think (that)

It seems to me (that)

2 Do you agree or disagree with the statement that there is no such thing as privacy anymore? What is your opinion on the amount of privacy we have today, as opposed to how much we had in the past?

In my opinion,

I think (that)

(But) even though

I (still) think (that)

It seems to me (that)

3 Is it right for companies to track what their employees do at work?

In my opinion,

I think (that)

(But) even though

I (still) think (that)

It seems to me (that)

4 Should employers be able to listen in on phone conversations that are not work related (student-teacher conferences, etc) if they are done on company-issued phones or at work or during work hours?

In my opinion,

I think (that)

(But) even though

I (still) think (that)

It seems to me (that)

5 Should companies be able to fire employees due to information they've found out from monitoring them? For example, should a company be able to fire someone for having left work early if they used a GPS device to discover that the employee left early?

In my opinion,

I think (that)

(But) even though

I (still) think (that)

It seems to me (that)

6 What do you think will happen in the future? Will there be even more intense monitoring, or will people start demanding governments make laws to limit such monitoring?

In my opinion,

I think (that)

(But) even though

I (still) think (that)

It seems to me (that)

PAIR WORK

Find a partner and take turns creating opinion runs. In your opinion runs, be sure to use the acknowledging and minimizing counterarguments II strategy. Try to speak for 60 seconds without stopping.

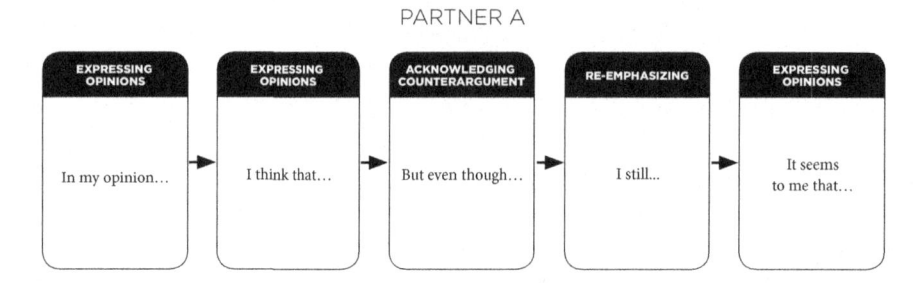

PARTNER A

EXPRESSING OPINIONS	EXPRESSING OPINIONS	ACKNOWLEDGING COUNTERARGUMENT	RE-EMPHASIZING	EXPRESSING OPINIONS
In my opinion…	I think that…	But even though…	I still…	It seems to me that…

CONVERSATION GAME

Divide into groups of 3-6. Discuss the preceding topic. Choose one person as your leader. Attempt to discuss and answer all questions. Use as many cards as you can. Record your score on a scorecard (Appendix E).

CONFIRMING INTERPRETATIONS

OBJECTIVES
- Introduce expressions for confirming interpretations, correcting misunderstandings, and affirming restatements
- Practice confirming interpretations, correcting misunderstandings, and affirming restatements
- Practice rephrasing

Often in conversations, we do no understand what our co-conversationalists have said and so it is necessary to ask them to rephrase their statements. We learned how to do this in Chapter 4. Another way to check understanding is to rephrase what we think the other person said.

In the first part of this chapter, we will learn to rephrase what others have said and affirm that what others think that we said is correct. Affirming means telling the other person their rephrasing is correct. In the second part of the chapter, we will learn to tell others that their rephrasing of our statements is not correct through correcting misunderstanding. In the third part of the chapter, we'll expand on correcting misunderstandings by rephrasing our own statements for our co-conversationalists with rephrasing phrases.

Expressions

Confirmation Requests

Would I be correct in saying (that)…
Basically, what you're saying is (that)…
Correct me if I'm wrong, but what you're saying is (that)…
Correct me if I'm wrong, but what you mean is (that)…

Affirmations

That's (exactly) what I meant.
That's what I said.
That's right.

Correcting Misunderstandings
  That's not (exactly) what I meant.
  That isn't quite what I meant.
  I think you misunderstood me.

Turn-Taking with Confirming Understanding & Affirming

Turn-taking with confirming understanding and affirming works similarly to the other types of turn-taking we have seen in this program. When one person expresses something that another individual does not understand, anyone in the conversation can attempt to restate what the first person has said. If the rephrasing is correct, the first person can affirm that the rephrasing is correct.

PAIR WORK

Find a partner and practice making statements about the topic above. Partner A should use opinion phrases to express an opinion, then partner B should attempt to rephrase what partner A has said using a confirming affirmation card. Finally, partner A should affirm that the rephrasing is correct. After practicing this several times, switch roles.

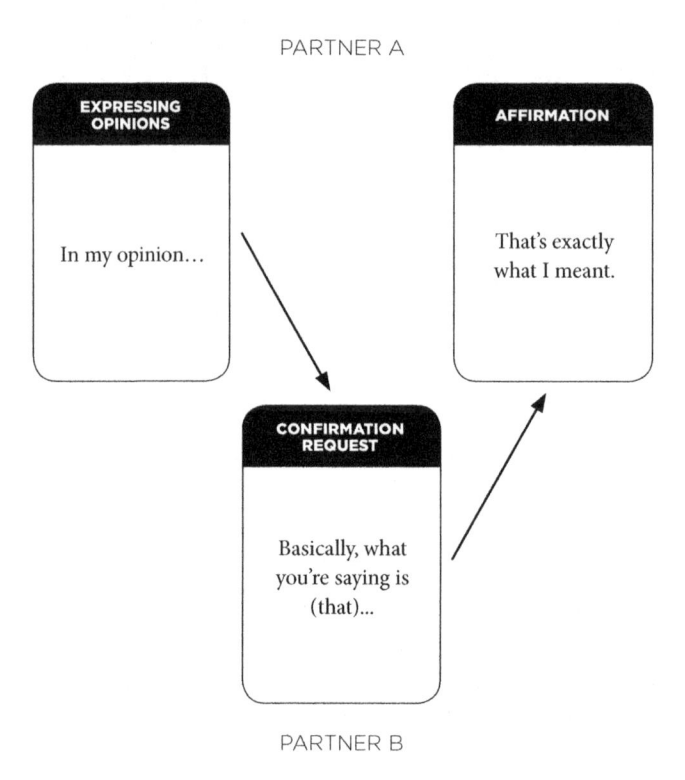

PARTNER A

EXPRESSING OPINIONS
In my opinion…

AFFIRMATION
That's exactly what I meant.

CONFIRMATION REQUEST
Basically, what you're saying is (that)…

PARTNER B

SAMPLE DIALOGUE

A: **In my opinion**, **I think** that having too much information has really paralyzed our ability to make decisions and to be creative.

B: **Would I be correct in saying that** you think that having too much information has been harmful?

A: **That's what I meant**.

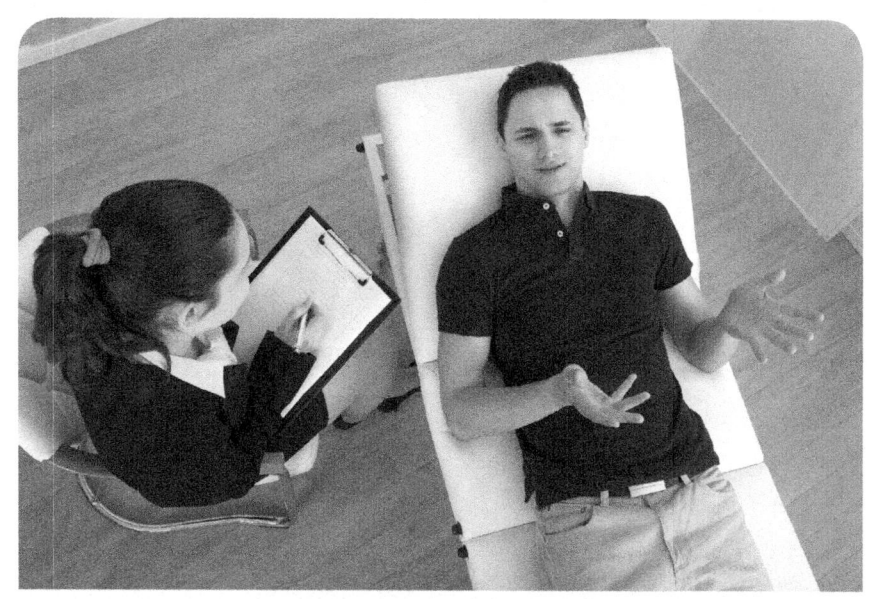

TOPIC #20: PSYCHOTHERAPY

Read the passage below and answer the questions. Answer each question thoroughly. Be sure to write about ideas that you may not be sure about so that you can use weak opinion phrases.

Psychotherapy is the process through which individuals can become aware of their motives, feelings, thoughts, actions and perceptions, and thereby change their behaviors. The basic premise of psychotherapy is that we all have behaviors that we learned in childhood. These behaviors, however, may not be beneficial to us in our adult lives. Nevertheless, because we are unaware of our behaviors, they will remain unchanged. Changing them is difficult.

In psychotherapy, an individual meets regularly with a therapist. They explore issues in one's life and attempt to discover why the individual behaves in particular ways. New ways of behaving are suggested and tried out, and the individual can then see the benefits or disadvantages of behaving in new ways.

However, a great deal of stigma surrounds psychotherapy. Many believe that only people with severe mental illnesses can go to a therapist and thus do not see psychotherapy as beneficial to them. Some view psychotherapy for only people with serious problems, such as people who have committed mass murders or other serious crimes.

Nevertheless, many in the field of psychotherapy argue that anyone can use psychotherapy to change his or her life. In addition, many claim that we are all somewhat mentally ill because no one is completely aware of all his or her own actions and perceptions. In fact, most neuroscientists agree that approximately 95% of our thoughts are below the conscious level, so there must be some of these thoughts that we could benefit from learning more about.

1 What is your opinion on this topic?

2 How aware do you think you are of your behaviors? Why? Can you give us any examples?

3 Are humans able to change behaviors that we have learned from childhood? Why or why not?

4 What about hardened criminals? Can they be changed or "reformed" enough to enter society as normal people?

5 Is there a stigma surrounding psychotherapy in your country? How common is it to see a psychotherapist?

6 Should we try to remove some of the stigma surrounding psychotherapy?

CONVERSATION GAME

Divide into groups of 3-6. Discuss the preceding topic. Choose one person as your leader. Attempt to discuss and answer all questions. Record the number of cards you played in the chart below. Did you use at least two *confirmation request* cards if you were a participant? Set a higher goal for yourself for the next round.

Turn-Taking with Confirming Understanding and Correcting Misunderstanding

Our co-conversationalists are not always successful when we attempt to rephrase what other people have said. Thus, it is important we have a way to correct other people's misunderstandings of our statements. We can call this mechanism *correcting misunderstandings*. The memorized phrases that we use for this mechanism are very similar to the *rephrasing* phrases from Chapter 4. Otherwise, the turn-taking looks similar to turn-taking with *affirmation* phrases.

PAIR WORK

Find a partner and practice turn-taking with *correcting misunderstanding* phrases. Partner A can make statements about the effects of technology, and partner B can incorrectly rephrase these statements. Then, Partner A can correct the misunderstanding by rephrasing what s/he has already said. After practicing several times, switch roles.

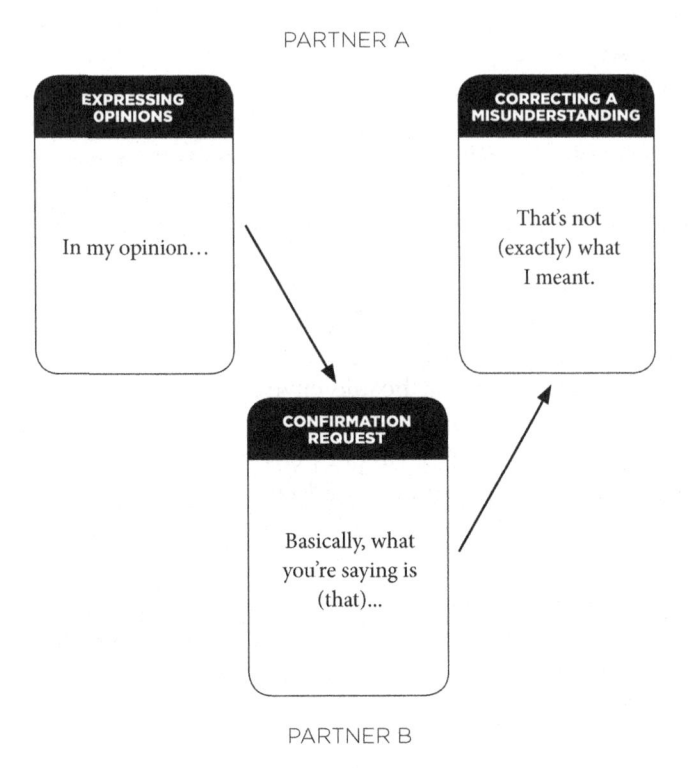

PARTNER A

EXPRESSING OPINIONS
In my opinion…

CORRECTING A MISUNDERSTANDING
That's not (exactly) what I meant.

CONFIRMATION REQUEST
Basically, what you're saying is (that)…

PARTNER B

TOPIC #21: IS PERSONALITY INHERITED?

Read the passage below and answer the questions.

Some people believe that personality is inherited. In other words, our personality traits are tied to our genes. Others disagree.

Research suggests that we have a genetic tendency for certain characteristics. In fact, some personality traits have been tied to genetics, including verbal ability, extroversion and introversion, the ability to enjoy large parties and public speaking, assert-iveness, and sociability.

Studies of twins have been influential in advancing the position that personality is inherited. In these studies, researchers have investigated differences in personality traits between identical twins and between these twins and their other siblings. They assert that identical twins have more in common with each other than they do with their other siblings. Furthermore, identical twins who were separated at birth and raised by adoptive parents were found to have more personality traits in common with their birth parents than they do with their adoptive parents.

However, many argue that we can change our personality with effort. They argue that, first of all, the environment plays a large role in our development. A child adopted into an abusive family will have personality traits, or behaviors, that enable him or her to survive in that hostile environment regardless of genetics. Likewise, others argue that birth order, the order in which you were born relative to your other siblings, plays a large role in our personalities. Firstborn children are often outgoing and trendsetters. Youngest children are often thought of as spoiled, middle children as problematic, and only children are often very mature and leaders, yet selfish.

1 In your opinion, do you think that personality is inherited, or does environment play a larger role in our formation?

2 Can we change our personality? If so, how, and how much can be changed?

3 What are the most important environmental influences (family, school, culture, language, education, etc.) on our personalities? Why?

4 What is the role of birth order in the formation of personality?

CONVERSATION GAME

Divide into groups of 3-6. Discuss the preceding topic. Choose one person as your leader. Use at least two confirmation requests and affirmation phrases as possible. Attempt to discuss and answer all questions. Use as many cards as possible.

Recording and Reflecting
In the chart below, record the number of cards played. Sort them by color. Assess your performance. Did you use at least two *confirmation request* cards if you were a participant? Records your score on a scorecard.

Softening the Blow and Buying Time with Rephrasing
One way to buy time and at the same time soften the blow is to add a rephrasing card after some of the correcting misunderstanding phrases. We typically pause briefly between the correcting misunderstanding phrase and the rephrasing phrase.

PAIR WORK

Work with a partner on mastering the strategy of buying time and softening the blow by adding a rephrasing phrase after a correcting misunderstanding phrase. Partner A can begin by expressing an opinion about the above topic, and partner B can attempt to incorrectly rephrase what partner A has said. Partner A can then correct the misunderstanding and then rephrase it. Switch roles after you have practiced this several times.

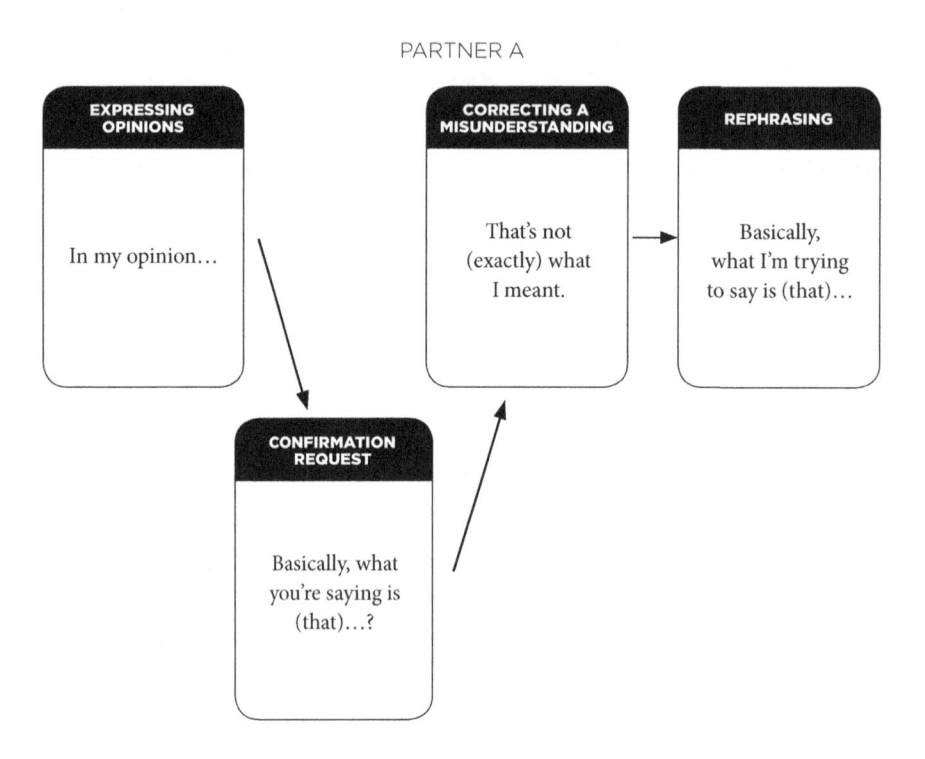

PARTNER A

EXPRESSING OPINIONS

In my opinion…

CONFIRMATION REQUEST

Basically, what you're saying is (that)…?

CORRECTING A MISUNDERSTANDING

That's not (exactly) what I meant.

REPHRASING

Basically, what I'm trying to say is (that)…

TOPIC #22: MOOD DISORDERS AND CREATIVITY

Read the passage below and answer the questions.

VOCABULARY

bi-polar - a mental condition/illness during which individuals cycle between being very happy and very sad

prescribe - to make an official order so a patient can purchase drugs. Typically, a doctor prescribes medicine for a patient.

anti-depressant - a drug that helps relieve the symptoms of depression

manic - periods of excessive energy, typically marked by happiness

depressed/depression - sad or sadness

Since at least the time of the Ancient Greeks, there has been a link between genius and mental illness. Great thinkers and philosophers were often seen as unique or strange, and having a mental illness was not viewed negatively, at least not by everyone. Socrates, for example, thought that mental illnesses were blessings bestowed by the gods; thus, those with mental conditions should not feel shameful, and no treatment was necessary to 'cure' them of these gifts. Throughout history there have been several creative geniuses who were said to have had mood disorders, including Beethoven, Virginia Woolf, Hemingway, Newton, and Schumann.

While there are various types of mental illnesses, those related to mood disorders—or cycling through depressed times and happy times—are most associated with creativity. The most often cited of these conditions is bipolarity—a condition under which an individual cycles between extremely happy, or manic, and extremely sad, or depressed, periods. During the depressed portion of the cycle, an individual may be completely incapacitated to the point of being unable to get out of bed. During the manic periods, on the other hand, the individual may be extremely productive and creative. S/he may think of new solutions to old problems, produce creative work such as painting or writing, or, in general, think of new ways to do things. Bi-polars are often very creative in their manic states. Bi-polar means there are two poles, a very depressed pole during which time the individual has difficulty doing anything, and manic, during which time the person has an extreme amount of energy. Maniacs have a great deal of energy and creativity during their manic phase—in fact, it is during this time that they are able to be very creative—they may produce a great deal of work, or come up with new solutions to problems, etc.

Some people have linked creativity to mental illness. In other words, people who may have certain mental illnesses may be more creative than 'normal' people, or people who have fewer mental issues. Various medications exist to help bi-polars keep a more level state of mind, but taking such medications comes at a cost: by eliminating the highs and lows of the bi-polar condition, individuals may also lose (some of their) creative ability. Thus, many bi-polars and others who are prescribed drugs don't take them because they miss the 'highs' and creative moments of their conditions. Some famous artists, in fact, avoid treatment because they are afraid it will affect their creativity. Some famous singers and actors refuse to go to because they believe it will affect their creativity.

1 What is your opinion?

2 Where does creativity come from? Are people with mental illnesses necessarily more creative than 'normal' people?

3 Are you a creative person? If so, are there times during which you are more creative or less creative?

4 Socrates believed that mental illness was a gift from the gods and should not be treated. Do you agree or disagree with this statement?

5 Which is more important, controlling mental illnesses such as depression and bi-polarity or allowing for creativity even though this might risk the individual becoming suicidal?

CONVERSATION GAME

Divide into groups of 3-6. Discuss the preceding topic. Choose one person as your leader. Attempt to discuss and answer all questions. Use at least two *confirmation requests*. Use as many cards as you can. Sort your cards by color and record the number used. Total your score. Assess your performance and set a goal for future games.

ALIGNING WITH OTHERS

OBJECTIVES
- Align with the social actions of other speakers
- Transform disagreement, agreement, avoiding a question, asking for repetition, and inviting participation statements into aligning statements
- Use 'yeah,' 'too,' 'either,' 'also,' and 'as well,' correctly in aligning statements
- Align with other aligning statements

In the previous chapters, we've learned new phrases and combined them to create a wide range of conversational moves and strategies. In this chapter, instead of combining, we will transform most of the phrases as we attempt the move *align with others*. When we align with others, we agree with others *socially*. In other words, we mirror the social action that they are completing, not necessarily the meaning of their words. Thus, for example, if another player is disagreeing or agreeing, we can align with this disagreement or agreement, but we can also align with asking others to repeat themselves, avoiding a question, or even inviting participation.

Each aligning move will require an aligning expression and card as well as the expression and card that we are aligning with. When we make an aligning statement, we use the exact same phrase that the person we are aligning with said plus 'yeah' and perhaps another word such as 'either' or 'too' in them. All aligning cards will look alike and contain all possible modifications we can make to another's phrase to make it an aligning phrase, but transformations may vary.

Expressions
Yeah … either/also/too/as well

Aligning with Third-Person Statements

The simplest aligning move is to align with a third-person phrase. There are several third-person agreement phrases (right, that's a good point, good point, exactly) and avoiding a question phrases (good question, that's a good question, that's a difficult question, that's an interesting question).

TOPIC #23: UNIDENTIFIED FLYING OBJECTS (UFOS)

Read the passage below and answer the questions.

> For centuries, humans have claimed to have seen unidentified flying objects, or UFOs. In 1450 BC, an ancient Egyptian Pharaoh, Tutmose III, claimed to have seen "circles of fire" brighter than the sun that gradually disappeared as they went upward in the sky. In 99BC, the Roman author Julius Obsequens described a shield-like round object which disappeared in the sky. And in 1235, Japanese General Yoritsume reported seeing circle-like objects moving about in the sky. Much art and architecture from ancient times depicts UFOs.
>
> Recently, more and more people claim to have seen UFOs. In fact, from about the 1880s to the present, many people have been claiming to have seen UFOs. Perhaps the most significant was the crew of a United Airlines plane who claimed to have seen nine disc-like objects. Some claim that UFOs are here to help humankind and that there are more sightings now because humankind has come to a critical point in its history and needs more help.
>
> Also, some claim that a UFO crashed in New Mexico near Roswell. They claim that the US government has held dead alien bodies and technology from the spacecrafts. In fact, they claim that the US military has used technology from the spacecraft to build military vehicles.
>
> Today, farmers occasionally find that their crops have been flattened into circle-like patterns overnight. Many claim that a UFO has visited and landed in their crop space. Others, however, say that this is the actions of humans. A couple of guys in England confirmed that for years they had been making crop circles with merely wire and measuring devices. Still, some insist that not all crop circles are made by humans.

1 What do you think about UFOs?

2 Do you believe that these historical sightings of UFOs are real or not real? Do you know of any other historical sightings?

3 Why are there more recent sightings today? Is this a fad, or are aliens really trying to help us?

4 Is the US government or other governments hiding UFO technology from us?

5 Are crop circles proof of the existence of aliens? Why or why not?

6 How do people in your country typically view UFOs?

....

....

....

PAIR WORK

Work with the partner on the above strategy. Pull all third-person *agreement*, *disagreement* and *avoiding a question* cards from the deck. Partner A should simply read the statement on the card, and partner B should align with that statement using 'yeah' plus a third-person statement. Once partner B has used all the third-person cards, switch roles.

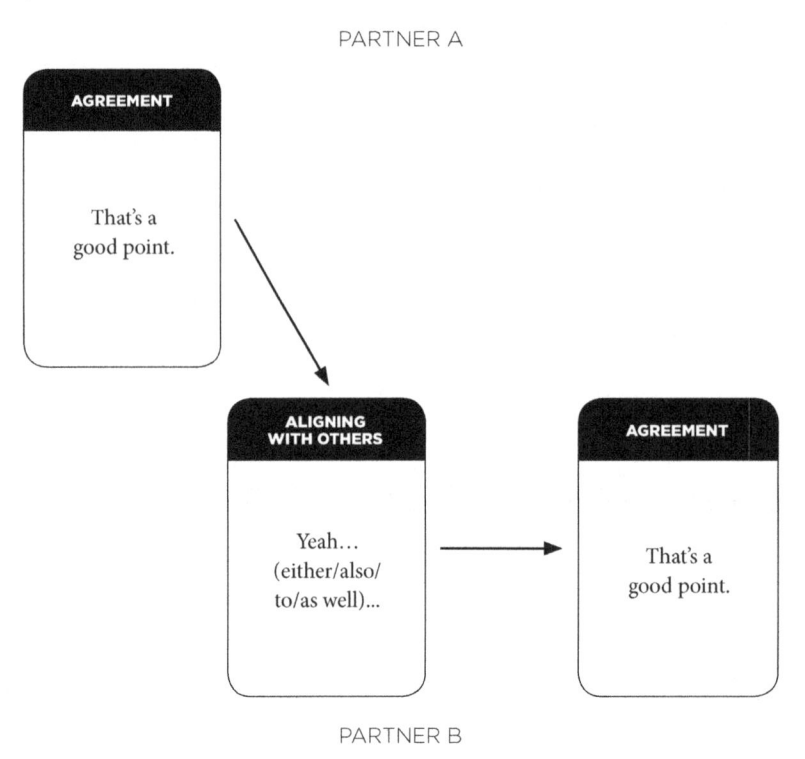

PARTNER A

[AGREEMENT card: That's a good point.] → [ALIGNING WITH OTHERS card: Yeah… (either/also/to/as well)…] → [AGREEMENT card: That's a good point.]

PARTNER B

SAMPLE DIALOGUE

    A: *That's right*.

    B: *Yeah, that's a good point*.

    A: *I couldn't agree with you more*.

    B: *Yeah, exactly*.

    A: *That's an interesting question*.

    B: *Yeah, that's a good question*.

    A: *That's a good point*.

    B: *Yeah, good point*.

CONVERSATION GAME

Form groups of 4-6 and discuss the above topic. Try to use as many alignment cards as possible.

Aligning with Positive First-Person Statements

Another aligning move can be made with positive first-person statements. These are statements that contain 'I' and do not contain words like 'not' or 'never.' Positive first-person statements include opinions [I think (that), I feel (that), I believe (that), It seems to me (that)], agreement (I agree, I feel the same way), and disagreement (I'm sorry, but I disagree, I disagree). To make an aligning statement, we place 'yeah' at the beginning of the statement and can optionally insert 'also' after the subject or 'too' or 'as well' at the end of the entire statement.

TOPIC #24: GHOSTS

Read the passage below and answer the questions.

> Every culture seems to have beliefs or myths about ghosts. However, not all beliefs are the same. In the West, there are two prevalent beliefs. First, many people believe that ghosts are the spirits of troubled humans. In other words, ghosts are the spirits of people who died before they were able to finish some business, so they have stayed on the earth to try to settle matters. For example, the spirits of people who were murdered may remain on the earth to seek revenge. Criminals may stay on the earth to avoid going to Hell. Second, scientists believe that ghosts do not exist or that perhaps humans have energy, and when a human dies, some energy may be left behind. This energy may cause unusual things to happen.
>
> Yet others believe that ghosts simply do not exist. They believe that because there is no conclusive evidence that ghosts exist, they must not be real. Some people become excited about the idea of ghosts and so they think they see and hear things, but this is merely their imaginations going wild.

1 What is your opinion on this topic?

2 If you believe in ghosts, how do you think they are formed?

3 Do people who want to believe in ghosts let their imagination go wild and see things that aren't really there? Why?

4 What does your culture think about ghosts? How does this compare with Western thought?

5 Do you believe that ghosts exist? Why or why not?

GROUP WORK: ALSO, TOO & AS WELL

Have the entire class form a circle. Everyone should separate the first-person cards out of the deck. Decide on the first person to start the game. This person should either express an opinion about *ghosts*, or simply make an agreement or disagreement statement. The person to this person's right should make an aligning statement with *also*. The next person to the right should then make an aligning statement with *too*, and then the following person should make a statement with *as well*. The very next person can make any agreement, disagreement, or opinion statement, and then the cycle should continue. Each person that makes a mistake should be taken out of the group, and the last person in the group, or the person who runs out of cards first (whichever comes first) wins.

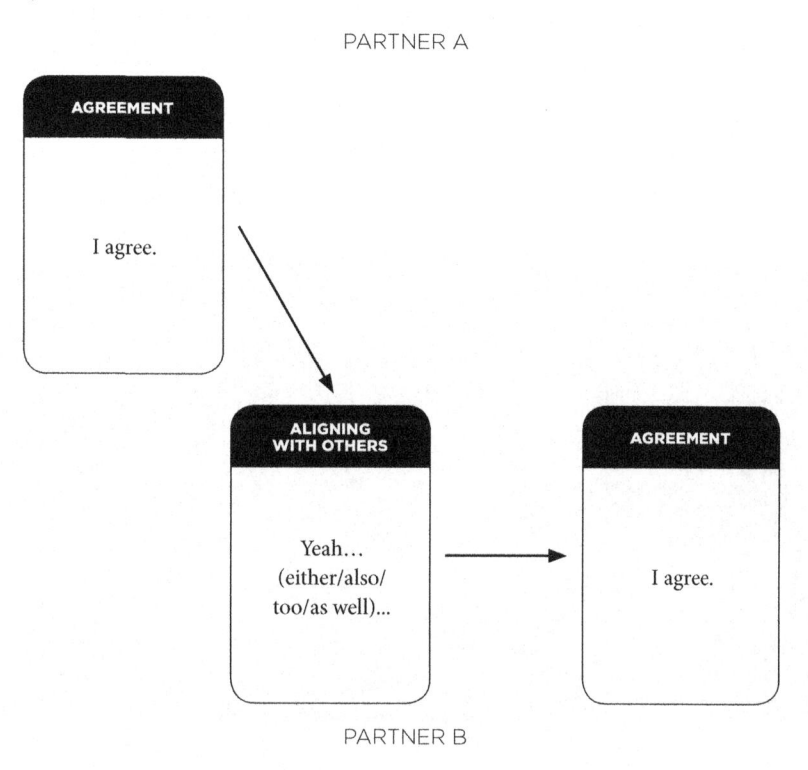

PARTNER A

AGREEMENT

I agree.

ALIGNING WITH OTHERS

Yeah… (either/also/too/as well)…

AGREEMENT

I agree.

PARTNER B

SAMPLE DIALOGUE

A: **_I think_** that this is an interesting topic

B: **_Yeah_**, **_I also think_** this topic is interesting.

C: **_Yeah_**, **_I think_** this is an interesting topic **_too_**.

D: **_Yeah_**, **_I believe_** this is a thought-provoking idea as well.

A: **_I'm not so sure about that_**.

B: **_Yeah, I also disagree_**.

C: **_Yeah, I disagree too_**.

D: **_Yeah, I'm sorry, but I disagree as well_**.

THE CONVERSATION GAME   **103**

CONVERSATION GAME

Form groups of 4-6 and discuss the above topic. Try to use as many alignment cards as possible. Optionally, play two alignment cards (for an extra point) if you use *also, too,* or *as well*. Afterwards, sort your cards and record them in the chart below.

Aligning with Negative First-Person Statements

A third aligning move can be made with negative first-person statements. A negative first-person statement is a statement that contains either 'I' or 'me' as well as a negative adverb, usually 'not' or 'never.' Negative first-person statements include opinions (I can't helping thinking (that)), agreement (I've never thought of it that way, I couldn't agree with you more), disagreement (I'm not so sure about that, I'm not sure I agree with that), and asking for repetition (I don't quite follow you).

To make a negative first-person statement an aligning one, we place 'yeah' before the statement, and then we must add 'also' after the subject or add 'either' at the end of the entire statement. Note that we can only use 'also,' 'either,' and 'as well' if we are using the exact same statement the previous person said.

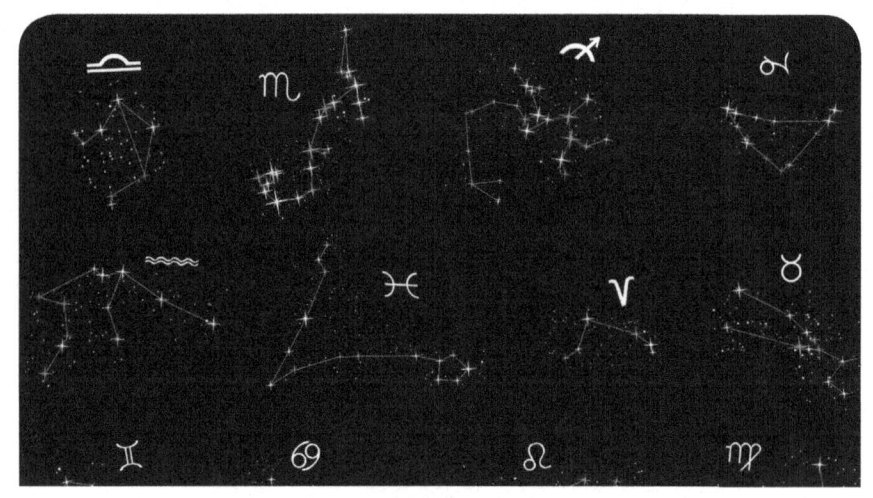

TOPIC #25: ASTROLOGICAL PROPHECY

Read the passage below and answer the questions.

VOCABULARY

startling - *surprising*
stargazer - *someone who watches the stars*
doomsayer - *one who predicts the end of the world*
coincidence - *something that happens by chance*

Prophecy is the ability to predict the future. For thousands of years, humans have attempted to predict the future by examining the movement of the stars and the planets. While there are many skeptics to astrological prophecy, there have also been some startlingly accurate predictions made by stargazers.

In the 1500s, a Frenchman named Nostradamus made a range of predictions, many of which doomsayers tie to specific historical events from the French revolution to the bombing of Hiroshima and Nagasaki. However, he wrote in a poetic manner that made it difficult to interpret. Thus, for example, he wrote about the second antichrist as 'Hisler,' which many interpret to have been Hitler, but others that 'Hisler' references the river Danube. Nostradamus also wrote about the beginning of World War III, which would start with the "division of two twins" in the "new city." Nostradamus enthusiasts have interpreted this as the destruction of the twin towers in 2001, but others say the reference is too vague to attribute it to that particular incident.

But astrological prophecy was not only being done in Europe. Various Indians in the Americas were also tracking and predicting future events based on an elaborate calendar system, one that is much more accurate than our current system. The Aztecs, the rulers of central Mexico, had a calendar that repeated itself every 52 years. At the end of each 52-year cycle was a short five-day period that was considered very unlucky. On the unlucky five-day period of a particularly ominous 52-year period, the Spanish conqueror Hernan Cortez arrived at the Aztec Capitol. This date marked the end of this great empire. The Mayan calendar also had units of time larger than 52-year periods called bak'tuns. A bak'tun was 394 years. The ends of the last several of these bak'tuns have brought about various changes to the Mayan civilization including the end of the last great Mayan empire at Lake Peten, the abandonment of the great Mayan city of Chichen Itza, the unexplained abandonment of 100s of Mayan cities, the rise of many new Mayan cities from the influence of Teotihuacan, and the abandonment of the last Olmec cities.

However, there are still plenty of doubters to predicting the future through astrology. Some claim that if the future can indeed be predicted by tracking the stars, then humans would have no control and thus no responsibility for their actions as they are all predetermined anyways. Others say that due to the varying tilt of the earth, it is impossible to accurately track the stars, thus making any sort of prediction impossible. Finally, others believe that people who try to predict the future are just trying to scare us all.

1 What is your opinion on this topic?

2 What are your opinions on Nostradamus's predictions? Are his poetic verses accurate, or are they coincidence?

3 What's your opinion on the end of the Aztec civilization? Did the Mayan calendar predict the arrival of the Spaniards, or is this by accident?

....

....

....

4 Several major changes occurred at the beginning of new 394 day periods based on the Mayan calendar. Why do you think this is?

....

....

....

5 We are at the beginning of a new bak'tun. What changes do you think this will bring, if any?

....

....

....

6 Are people who try to predict the future trying to scare us, or are they trying to warn us of potential problems that we can avoid?

....

....

....

GROUP WORK: ALSO, TOO & AS WELL

Have the entire class form a circle. Everyone should separate the first-person cards out of the deck. Decide on the first person to start the game. This person should either express an opinion about astrological prophesy, or simply make an agreement or disagreement statement. The person to this person's right should make an aligning statement with *also*. The next person to the right should then make an aligning statement with *too*, and then the following person should make a statement with *as well*. The very next person can make any agreement, disagreement, or opinion statement, and then the cycle should continue. Each person that makes a mistake should leave the group, and the last person in the group, or the person who runs out of cards first (whichever comes first) wins.

106 ALIGNING WITH OTHERS

PARTNER A

ASKING FOR REPETITION

I don't quite follow you.

ALIGNING WITH OTHERS

Yeah… (either/also/ to/as well)…

ASKING FOR REPETITION

I don't quite follow you.

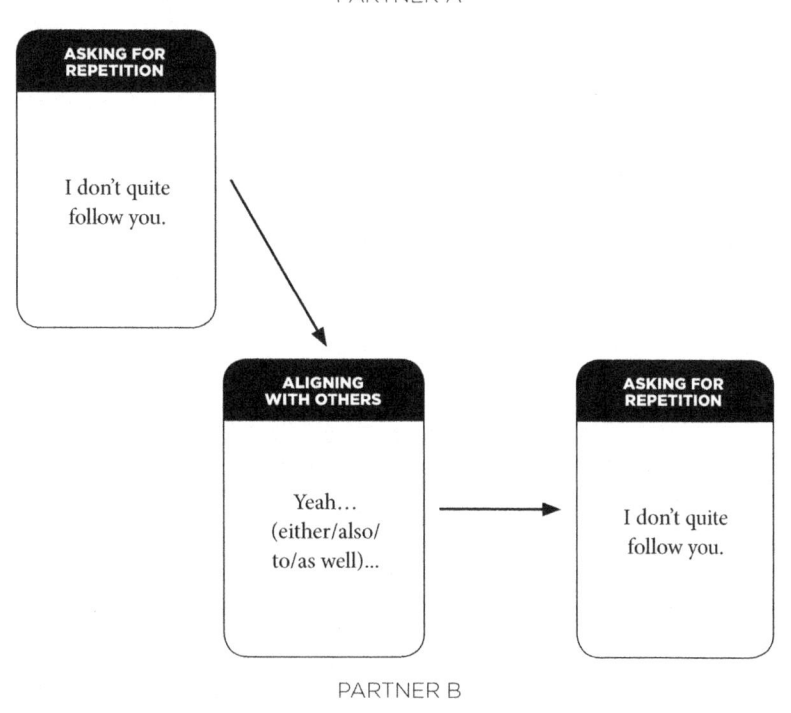

PARTNER B

SAMPLE DIALOGUE

A: *I don't quite follow you*.

B: *Yeah*, *I also don't quite follow you*.

C: *Yeah*, *I don't quite follow you either*.

A: *I couldn't agree with you more*.

B: *Yeah*, *I also couldn't agree with you more*.

C: *Yeah*, *I couldn't agree with you more either*.

A: *I've never thought of it that way*.

B: *Yeah*, *I've also never thought of it that way*.

C: *Yeah*, *I've never thought of it that way either*.

CONVERSATION GAME

Form groups of 4-6 and discuss the above topic. Try to use as many alignment cards as possible. Optionally, play two alignment cards (for an extra point) if you use *also, too,* or *as well*. Afterwards, record the numbers of each type of phrase you used below.

THE CONVERSATION GAME **107**

ASSESSING PROGRESS AND FURTHER PRACTICE

OBJECTIVES

- Assess progress
- Create a plan for future work
- Compare current conversation ability to initial ability

In this program, we've learned about and practiced using a wide range of conversation strategies, and we've extensively used cards to help scaffold our learning. Now, we'll have a conversation without cards to assess the progress we've made.

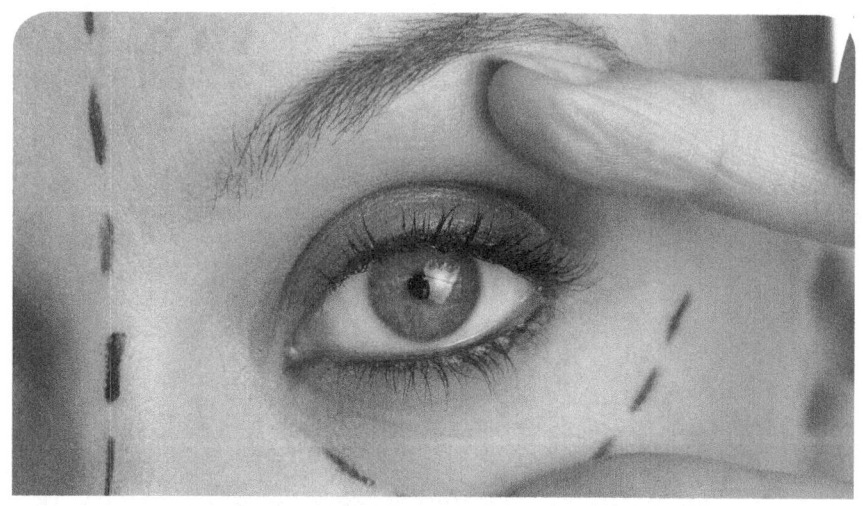

TOPIC #26: PLASTIC SURGERY

Read the passage below and answer the questions.

Plastic surgery has become quite popular. Initially, it was only for very rich people and movie stars. It was used to make them look younger and perhaps thinner. Now, however, plastic surgery is used by a wide range of people, rich and poor, to enhance appearance.

While plastic surgery has become more popular, it is still dangerous. It is an unnecessary operation that sometimes results in death. Also, while the surgery may have the intended effects, side effects may not present themselves for several years. For example, a woman who gets breast implants may be very happy with them for a few years, but if they start to leak, she will have to have them removed (and pay for the removal, usually), and the leaking can cause sickness or even death.

Others believe plastic surgery to be vain: it is for people who want to look good only and are not satisfied with how they look. Yet, people who are comfortable with themselves do not need to have plastic surgery. Beauty comes from happiness and confidence, not from physical looks. Still, those who spend time and money on plastic surgery believe the cost and risks are well worth it.

1 What is your opinion on this topic?

2 Do you think plastic surgery is dangerous? If so, how dangerous is it?

3 Where does beauty come from?

4 Is plastic surgery common in your country? Why or why not? How do people view plastic surgery in your country?

5 If you had the money, would you get plastic surgery? Why?

PAIR WORK

Find a partner and spend 5-10 minutes discussing this topic. You may discuss the topic itself, or you might decide to discuss what kinds of moves and strategies you can use in a conversation about *plastic surgery*.

CONVERSATION GAME

Work in groups of 4-6. Make sure you have some sort of recording device to record the conversation. Each person may have his/her own recording device, or the group may share the device. Choose a leader, and discuss the preceding topic. Try to use as many conversational strategies as possible, but without using your cards.

	Diagnostic	*Final Evaluation*	*Ratio: Final/Diagnostic*
Number of turns:			
Number of words per turn:			
Number of mistakes:			
Mistakes/total words:			
Mistakes/number of turns:			

Written Assignment: Final Evaluation

Listen to and transcribe your conversation. Try to transcribe exactly what you've said, including any grammar or wording mistakes, pronunciation mistakes, long pauses, hesitations, and repetitions. After you've transcribed it, have your teacher help you find all wording and grammar mistakes. For a simple diagnostic, you can count the following:

We can use this chart to assess our improvement over the course of the program. By dividing the final score by the initial score, we should come up with our percent change. Keep in mind, that acquiring conversational ability is not just a linear process, so all the numbers above may not be positive. For example, we might have a lower number of words per turn than we did initially. This is not necessarily negative, especially if we were only speaking when we could speak at length. Shorter, more concise utterances are more common in conversation than long, drawn-out monologues. Furthermore, if there was not a separate focus on improving pronunciation and grammar errors, it is quite likely those would not improve on their own.

Individual Written Assignment

Write a reflection paper on your experience with this program. Use the above chart to help you. Also, and importantly, if you regularly have conversations in English outside of class, discuss how your experience in those conversations has changed, if at all.

APPENDIX A
EXTRA PRACTICE

Further Practice
There are easy ways to extend the chapters in order to get more practice with the phrases and moves in each chapter.

Write your own Topic
Research a topic you are interested in, perhaps one related to the theme of the chapter. Write a brief (two to five) paragraph summary of the topic. Include both sides of the argument. Write four to five questions for discussion, the first of which can be "What is your opinion of this topic?" Give your fellow students your topic and time to read the topic before beginning a conversation game. Lead the topic you wrote.

Speed Rounds
Form groups of 3-4 and prepare to discuss a topic, any topic. The topics you have already discussed are fine since this exercise is designed to help you master leader expressions. Choose a leader and begin the discussion, lead the topic as quickly as possible. Give participants no more than one minute to discuss each question. You should finish the topic in five minutes. Each participant should use a minimum of ten cards, and the leader should use all leader cards. Optionally, the groups can race each other and see which group is the fastest. After you have finished, pick a new topic or the same topic and discuss again, choosing a new leader. Make sure everyone gets to practice being leader at least once.

Restricted Play
Form groups of 3-4 and prepare to discuss a topic, any topic. This can be a new topic that you have prepared or a topic from this book that you have already discussed. Choose one person as the leader. The leader should use leader cards and participant cards as shown below. Shuffle all participant cards that you have used thus far. Place eight random cards on the desk/table you are using. Begin the discussion. You may use any of the eight cards in front of you. Once you have played a card, replace it with a random card from the deck. This should force you to use all expressions, not just the ones you are most comfortable with.

EXAMPLE OF PLACEMENT

INTERRUPTION	MANAGING THE CONVERSATION	MANAGING THE CONVERSATION	MOVING THE CONVERSATION ALONG
I don't quite follow you	I couldn't agree with you more.	I think (that)...	In my opinion,...

INTERRUPTION	MANAGING THE CONVERSATION	MANAGING THE CONVERSATION	MOVING THE CONVERSATION ALONG
Let me put it this way...	Could you speak a little more loudly?	That's right.	Exactly.

APPENDIX B
TOPICS

Chapter 1   *Public Smoking Bans*

Chapte 2   *Learning a Language*
World Language
Standardized English Tests

Chapter 3   *Astrology*
Feng Shui
Dreams

Chapter 4   *The Growing Problem of Obesity*
Obesity in the Workplace
Fat Tax

Chapter 5   *Invasive Species and Exotic Pets*
Global Warming
The Ecological Impact of Green Energy

Chapter 6   *School Choice*
Home Schooling
School Uniforms

Chapter 7   *Face-Recognition Software*
Google Earth
Workplace Surveillance

Chapter 8   *Psychotherapy*
Is Personality Inherited?
Mood Disorders and Creativity

Chapter 9   *Unidentified Flying Objects (UFOs)*
Ghosts
Astrological Prophecy

Chapter 10   *Plastic Surgery*

APPENDIX C
PARTICIPANT CARDS

The following pages contain cards with the expressions in the chapters. You should copy and cut the cards for each chapter as you go, or copy and cut them all at once. At the top of each card is a label which tells you what kind of conversation move it is. Many teachers and students have benefited from copying different conversation moves on different colored paper. Optimally, the cards would be copied on card stock as they will be used repeatedly as you progress through the book.

EXPRESSING OPINIONS	**EXPRESSING OPINIONS**	**EXPRESSING OPINIONS**	**EXPRESSING OPINIONS**
I think (that)…	I think (that)…	I think (that)…	I think (that)…
EXPRESSING OPINIONS	**EXPRESSING OPINIONS**	**EXPRESSING OPINIONS**	**EXPRESSING OPINIONS**
My sense is (that)…	I feel (that)…	I feel (that)…	I feel (that)…
EXPRESSING OPINIONS	**EXPRESSING OPINIONS**	**EXPRESSING OPINIONS**	**EXPRESSING OPINIONS**
In my opinion…	In my opinion…	I can't help thinking…	I can't help thinking…
EXPRESSING OPINIONS	**EXPRESSING OPINIONS**	**EXPRESSING OPINIONS**	**EXPRESSING OPINIONS**
In my opinion…	It seems to me (that)…	It seems to me (that)…	It seems to me (that)…

AGREEMENT	**AGREEMENT**	**AGREEMENT**	**AGREEMENT**
I feel the same way.	I feel the same way.	I agree.	I agree.
AGREEMENT	**AGREEMENT**	**AGREEMENT**	**AGREEMENT**
You're right.	You're right.	Right.	Right.
AGREEMENT	**AGREEMENT**	**AGREEMENT**	**AGREEMENT**
That's a good point.	That's a good point.	I've never thought of it that way.	I've never thought of it that way.
AGREEMENT	**AGREEMENT**	**AGREEMENT**	**AGREEMENT**
Exactly.	Good point.	I couldn't agree with you more.	I couldn't agree with you more.

THE CONVERSATION GAME

DISAGREEMENT	DISAGREEMENT	DISAGREEMENT	DISAGREEMENT
I hate to disagree with you, but don't you think…	I hate to disagree with you, but don't you think…	I'm sorry, but I disagree.	I'm not so sure about that.

DISAGREEMENT	DISAGREEMENT	DISAGREEMENT	DISAGREEMENT
I'm not so sure about that.	Yes, but don't you think…	I see your point, but don't you think…	I see your point, but don't you think…

INTRODUCTION	INTRODUCTION	INTRODUCTION	INTRODUCTION
Our topic today is…	I'd like to know what you think about…	What's your opinion on this topic?	Would anyone like to comment?

CONCLUSION	CONCLUSION	CONCLUSION	CONCLUSION
I'd like to summarize our discussion so far.	Let's wind up our conversation, I'll take one more comment.	I'm sorry our time is up.	Thank you for your participation.

ASKING FOR REPETITION	**ASKING FOR REPETITION**	**ASKING FOR REPETITION**	**ASKING FOR REPETITION**
Could you speak a little more loudly?	Could you speak a little more loudly?	Could you speak a little more slowly?	Could you speak a little more slowly?
ASKING FOR REPETITION	**ASKING FOR REPETITION**	**ASKING FOR REPETITION**	**ASKING FOR REPETITION**
(I'm sorry) I don't quite follow you.	(I'm sorry) I don't quite follow you.	I'm afraid I'm not clear on what you meant by that.	I'm afraid I'm not clear on what you meant by that.
REPHRASING	**REPHRASING**	**REPHRASING**	**REPHRASING**
Let me put it this way…	Let me put it this way…	Let me put it this way…	Let me put it this way…
REPHRASING	**REPHRASING**	**REPHRASING**	**REPHRASING**
Basically, what I'm trying to say is…	Basically, what I'm trying to say is…	Basically, what I'm saying is…	Basically, what I'm saying is…

THE CONVERSATION GAME

ELICITING PARTICIPATION	ELICITING PARTICIPATION	ELICITING PARTICIPATION	ELICITING PARTICIPATION
Does anyone else have a comment?	Now let's hear from (name).	Now let's hear from (name).	What do you think (name)?

ELICITING PARTICIPATION	ELICITING PARTICIPATION	ELICITING PARTICIPATION	ELICITING PARTICIPATION
Would anyone like to say something about that?	Would anyone like to say something about that?	Would anyone like to add something?	Would anyone like to add something?

AVOIDING A QUESTION	AVOIDING A QUESTION	AVOIDING A QUESTION	AVOIDING A QUESTION
Good question.	That's a good question.	That's a good question.	That's a good question, I'm glad you brought it up.

AVOIDING A QUESTION	AVOIDING A QUESTION	AVOIDING A QUESTION	AVOIDING A QUESTION
That's a difficult question.	That's an interesting question.	That's an interesting question.	You've brought up a very interesting point/idea.

OBJECTIVES

MANAGING THE CONVERSATION	**MANAGING THE CONVERSATION**	**MANAGING THE CONVERSATION**	**MANAGING THE CONVERSATION**
I think we're getting off the subject.	I think we're getting off the subject.	I think we're getting off the subject.	I think we're getting off the subject.

MANAGING THE CONVERSATION	**MANAGING THE CONVERSATION**	**MANAGING THE CONVERSATION**	**MANAGING THE CONVERSATION**
Let's try to stick to the topic of this discussion.	Let's try to stick to the topic of this discussion.	Let's try to stick to the topic of this discussion.	Let's try to stick to the topic of this discussion.

INTERRUPTION	**INTERRUPTION**	**INTERRUPTION**	**INTERRUPTION**
Excuse me, may/can I interrupt you for a second?	Excuse me, may/can I interrupt you for a second?	May/can I interrupt you for a second?	Let me interrupt just for a second.

KEEPING THE CONVERSATION MOVING	**KEEPING THE CONVERSATION MOVING**	**KEEPING THE CONVERSATION MOVING**	**KEEPING THE CONVERSATION MOVING**
Let's move on to the next/last question.	Let's move on to the next/last question.	Let's move on to the next/last question.	Let's move on to the next/last question.

THE CONVERSATION GAME

MINIMIZING COUNTERARGUMENTS	**MINIMIZING COUNTERARGUMENTS**	**MINIMIZING COUNTERARGUMENTS**	**MINIMIZING COUNTERARGUMENTS**
(But) Even if...	(But) Even if...	(But) Even though...	(But) Even though...
RE-EMPHASIZING ONE'S OPINION	**RE-EMPHASIZING ONE'S OPINION**	**RE-EMPHASIZING ONE'S OPINION**	**RE-EMPHASIZING ONE'S OPINION**
I still...	I still...	I still...	I still...
CONFIRMATION REQUESTS	**CONFIRMATION REQUESTS**	**CONFIRMATION REQUESTS**	**CONFIRMATION REQUESTS**
Would I be correct in saying (that)...	Would I be correct in saying (that)...	Basically, what you're saying is (that)...	Basically, what you're saying is (that)...
CONFIRMATION REQUESTS	**CONFIRMATION REQUESTS**	**CONFIRMATION REQUESTS**	**CONFIRMATION REQUESTS**
Correct me if I'm wrong, but what you're saying is (that)...	Correct me if I'm wrong, but what you're saying is (that)...	Correct me if I'm wrong, but what you mean is (that)...	Correct me if I'm wrong, but what you mean is (that)...

AFFIRMATIONS	**AFFIRMATIONS**	**AFFIRMATIONS**	**AFFIRMATIONS**
That's (exactly) what I meant.	That's (exactly) what I meant.	That's what I said.	That's right.

CORRECTING MISUNDERSTANGINGS	**CORRECTING MISUNDERSTANGINGS**	**CORRECTING MISUNDERSTANGINGS**	**CORRECTING MISUNDERSTANGINGS**
That's not (exactly) what I meant.	That isn't quite what I meant.	That isn't quite what I meant.	I think you misunderstood me.

ALIGNING WITH OTHERS	**ALIGNING WITH OTHERS**	**ALIGNING WITH OTHERS**	**ALIGNING WITH OTHERS**
Yeah… (either/also/too/as well)…	Yeah… (either/also/too/as well)…	Yeah… (either/also/too/as well)…	Yeah… (either/also/too/as well)…

ALIGNING WITH OTHERS	**ALIGNING WITH OTHERS**	**ALIGNING WITH OTHERS**	**ALIGNING WITH OTHERS**
Yeah… (either/also/too/as well)…	Yeah… (either/also/too/as well)…	Yeah… (either/also/too/as well)…	Yeah… (either/also/too/as well)…

THE CONVERSATION GAME

APPENDIX D
TYPES OF EXPRESSIONS AND MOVES

Chapter 1
    Diagnostic

Chapter 2
    Opinion
    Agreement
    Disagreement
    Opening up the floor with agreement
    Buying time with 'In + I'

Chapter 3
    Introducing a topic
    Concluding a topic
    Keeping the conversation moving
    Introducing a topic
    Moving the discussion along
    Concluding conversations

Chapter 4
    Asking for repetition
    Rephrasing
    Turn-taking with asking for repetition and rephrasing
    Softening the blow with two repetition phrases
    Buying time with two rephrasing phrases + opinion

Chapter 5
    Eliciting participation
    Avoiding a question
    Turn-taking with eliciting participation and avoiding questions
    Buying time with avoiding the question + opinion
    Buying time with avoiding the question + 'In + I'

Chapter 6
    Managing the conversation
    Interruption
    Interrupting
    Going off on tangents and reining in tangents
    Interrupting + reining in tangents + moving the discussion along

Chapter 7
    Acknowledging and minimizing counterarguments
    Re-emphasizing one's opinion
    Opinion runs
    Acknowledging and minimizing hypothetical statements
    Acknowledging and minimizing real statements

Chapter 8
    Confirmation requests
    Affirmations
    Correcting misunderstandings
    Turn-taking with confirming understanding and affirming
    Turn-taking with confirming understanding and correcting misunderstanding
    Softening the blow and buying time with rephrasing

Chapter 9
    Aligning with others
    Aligning with third-person statements
    Aligning with positive first-person statements
    Aligning with negative first-person statements

Chapter 10
    Self-Evaluation

APPENDIX E
PHOTOCOPIABLE SCORE SHEET

Use all cards you have seen up to the current chapter. By the end of the program, you should be using all cards in each conversation game.

☐ **Opinion**
(Chapters 2-9)

☐ **Agreement**
(Chapters 2-9)

☐ **Disagreement**
(Chapters 2-9)

☐ **(Leader) Introduction**
(Chapter 3-9)

☐ **(Leader) Conclusion**
(Chapters 3-9)

☐ **(Leader) Keeping the Conversation Moving**
(Chapters 3-9)

☐ **Ask for Repetition**
(Chapters 4-9)

☐ **Rephrasing**
(Chapters 4-9)

☐ **Avoiding a Question**
(Chapters 5-9)

☐ **(Leader) Eliciting Participation**
(Chapters 5-9)

☐ **Interruption**
(Chapters 6-9)

☐ **(Leader) Managing the Conversation**
(Chapters 6-9)

☐ **Confirmation Request**
(Chapters 8-9)

☐ **Affirmation**
(Chapters 8-9)

☐ **Correcting Misunderstanding**
(Chapters 8-9)

☐ **Aligning**
(Chapter 9)

TOTAL ☐

Made in the USA
Middletown, DE
09 March 2022